BJ'S WHOLESALE CLUB:
Sales Are Down, But the Monkey Business Is Booming!

by
The Esteemed Dr. Zaius

Introduction

All the problems seem to be the same, no matter what store location we're speaking to workers at it's the same thing. Managers taking advantage of their workers, by changing hours, cutting hours, verbal abuse, etc...
- bjsworkers.blogspot

A meat manager resigned when his General Manager (GM) confronted him about out of date meat upon his return from leave while caring for his daughter diagnosed with cancer.

"Your shrink/salvage numbers are too low" the GM told the Produce Specialist. Or in this bizarro world situation, the General Damager. "Produce shrink/salvage is supposed to be 3-4 percent of sales. Yours is 1.2 percent", he said. "As a Produce Specialist, he thought I wasn't throwing away enough produce, and that my orders were so light that my shelves must've been empty. We took a walk to the floor, and he saw everything was full, and my cooler was adequately stocked. Regardless of what he saw, all he had on his mind was "the numbers". So none of that mattered.

"Everybody clock out and go home!", the NonFood Overnight Manager told all of the cashiers who were milling about the television section, talking instead of turning off the screens for the night. This came after the young lady stationed at the front door and denied a restroom break, broke down in front of him when he asked how she was doing. I came in before he did, and asked the same, and she told me she was alright. She transferred here from another club, drove a stand-up forklift [mechanical horse/chariot], and was a fantastic person and worker. But she needed to go to the daytime for personal reasons until she and her fiancee moved to another State. He stood at the door to give her that much needed break. Once she returned, he cleared house, undermining the daytime managers who were on duty.

"Why isn't the dock clear?" the Receiving and Inventory Control Manager asked the overnight receiver. "I was helping on the floor", he said. "Who told you to help on the floor?" she asked. "The Overnight Specialist did because he was alone and had a short staff. So he had me go to the floor once I finished unloading the Buriss truck and the 840". She replied back, "You can't leave the dock like this. It makes it hard on the daytime receiver. Now he has to clear the dock, which was your job, receive the trucks for this morning, and boom them up". Not once did she confront any of the Overnight Specialists whenever this happened. And it happened often, also at her previous club.

A team member from the night crew had a blow out while driving to work on the Interstate. Fortunately, he didn't have an accident. He called work to let the overnight specialists know about his situation, told them he would be late, and called Triple A. He got his car towed home, and then drove to work in his mother's car. A day or so late, he got a write up for being late. He took it to the GM to get the matter resolved. The GM responded by flatly telling him, "You could have called out. No one made you come to work."

"Get rid of that empty box there", the General Manager In Training (GMIT) told the asset protection team member at the front door who was checking receipts to verify purchases, as he casually walked outside. "Ok, I will", he replied. Moments later, the GMIT returned, saw the box, and grilled him about why it was still there. The team member told him he would pick up the box when he had time because at the moment, he was verifying purchases. Not liking what he heard, the GMIT firmly says, "Make sure you see me later. Don't clock out to go home before you do", as he angrily picks up the box and takes it with him.

"What happened to you last night?", the Overnight Food Manager asked, as he rolled up on me on his mechanical horse. Apparently, in addition to his designated managerial responsibilities, he had to do my section, and wasn't happy about it. I told him I was off. This was a huge deal, considering that a weekend night off for a member of the night crew was rarer then rare. That was unless they called out, requested it, were on vacation, or in my case, deserved it because he worked especially hard night after night, faithfully and consistently. He rode off on his chariot, "beep, beep, beep", the sound a large made when it was in reverse. I continued to "recover" my aisles, which was our shop talk for straightening. Then the Overnight NonFood Manager rolled up on his mechanical horse, jumped off, and asked the same question! Alright, now I'm hot! What sort of manager assumes a team member will be working? It never once crossed their minds to check the schedule.

"You're cleaning the meat cases now? Why are you doing that?" the meat manager asked his opening meat cutter. "I came in early to clean the cases because you told me to", the meat cutter retorts. The meat manager replies, "You know we have to get the place ready to open at 8 o'clock. And we have lots of meat to cut. I should write you up for this". The meat cutter flat out tells him, "If you do, I'll write on there that you were the one who told me to come in early and do it."

Table of Contents

Introduction ii

1. The Top Banana 1

2. The Monkey Method 7

3. Monkey Ways of Thinking 11

4. Bachelor Degree in Monkey Business 30

5. Masters Degree in Monkey Business 48

6. Flinging Poo at You 56

7. Monkey Wrench 68

8. Dial 911 84

9. Paid In Bananas 89

10. Monkey Hustle 105

11. Monkeying Around 112

12. Swinging from the Steel 121

Resources 129

Chapter One: The Top Banana

The stories you just read are all true. There are just some things you cannot make up when it comes to retail. We know the same goes for corporate, e.g. Scott Adams's Dilbert comic strip. Actually, it happens everywhere in both the private and public sector. But this time, we will focus on retail, and the #3 wholesale club in the country and world. It is #3, and will remain there.

Many of the employees named in the original blog may strongly disagree with what with other employees said about them...even if what was said was accurate. So as to not draw their ire, and risk them coming after me for libel or defamation, I partially redacted their names. Employees who posted the comments [in italics], or are familiar with those particular employees will know their identities.

Glassdoor is a website that allows current and former employees to voice their opinions, good, bad, or neutral about current and former employers. One scathing remark someone made about BJ's Wholesale Club was it was ran by a bunch of "failed grocery store managers". That statement wasn't wholly true, but seemed that way, especially after the influx of Winn Dixie and Publix management at one point.

THE TOP BANANA

In this book, you will find a collection of some of the most interesting and colorful posts from the bjsworkersblogspot. Who created the site is largely unknown. Some who posted to it thought BJ's upper management started it. Regardless of who did, the content provides tremendous insight as to why BJ's is ranked where it is, and definitely never again will be what it was when it began in Massachusetts in 1984.

BJ's would be an excellent place for Undercover Boss. Let the boss see how it feels to be one of two cashiers on duty because of payroll, and facing lines of members. The Front Line Supervisor (FLS) doesn't want to ring anyone up, and the managers are nowhere to be found. Or be the only employee in the deli when there is a line, and the next worker doesn't come in until after noon. Even worse, the next worker calls out, and a manager asks you to do a double. Maybe the boss could work at the front door in the winter, and freeze because management says they cannot cover their company uniform red shirts. There is also the option of making the boss work overnight, and have overzealous overnight specialists delight in dropping dozens of pallets for them to work, many which are unnecessary, while riding around all night on their mechanical horses, and refusing to help when they are short staffed. On the flip side, the boss could be made an overnight specialist who gets bombarded with overnight homework to do. Then the Assistant Manager Merchandise (AMM)/Senior Merchandising Manager/Senior Merchant or the GM comes in fresh from a good night's sleep and demands more work on top of the notes from the previous night. That causes overtime, and then at the end of the week, the Operations Manager aka OPS or Assistant Manager Operations (AMO), says to leave early or come in late before the week ends to get rid of the time. Or how about this? The GM

THE TOP BANANA

or Senior Merchant writes you up for the overtime he or she caused you to have. The boss could also be a Customer Service Membership Manager (CSSM or MSM) who is held accountable for customer service and membership sales, and gets written up when sales goals aren't met. A few months before I began this book, a beloved MSM quit after being written up/put on paper for low membership sales and renewals. He left for the bank, which will be a better fit for him. On a side note: BJ's has an unhealthy obsession with acronyms. Member Service Manager (MSM) used to be a senior position. Now it's a mid manager position with dual roles. BJ's renamed many operations with new titles when it transitioned to a new system called Mosaic. Why rename something just for the sake of renaming it? There are actually people paid well to do just that. Sometimes, they are people in newly created positions.[1] BJ's also consolidated and renamed positions after a mass culling in January 2016.

Someone is making money and big bonuses. So no matter how much management says sales are down, I know the monkey business is booming!

Let's take a look at reasons why current and former employees think BJ's can be much greater than it is. A fair warning. I left all the blog posts the way I found them; I made no corrections. So consider how much people use their cell phones, how auto complete works, and the fact that some people weren't English majors in college, or did that well in English in high school.

This company has to decide what it wants to be. Dose it want to be a warehouse club, a grocery store or a dept store. It sufferes from a Identity crisis, as seen by the many new programs that get implimented and then pushed to the side when a new idea

THE TOP BANANA

hits them. So far, they have failed to really stick with any program long enough to actually see them through to the end.

If BJ'S would follow Costco's game plan, they would be number 1 instead of Costco. Stop the griping, be glad you have a job, and if you are so unhappy, GO TO COSTCO.

if sales are up.. why is budget down?

So with all the sales increases you would think they would get more payroll to the clubs. Instead they cut hours more. How do they keep a straight face when saying " Member services, Members first!" and not have enough people to stock the shelves or check people out?

To the commentor of: To the person ho made the comment that "home office is on track" must be delusional. I am not delusional but you mis understand where I speak of in Home Office, I'm speaking of the top, **La** etc., don't think for a moment that they condon abuse of policies and procedures. However, old style managers who are without business degrees are in the system because they came up through the ranks, some starting as cart kids. No knock on what they've accomplished but some skills are taught in college that have more to do with running a business and have nothing to do with bull working in the clubs. For example; job descriptions are ignored at times to point where qualified applicants can't seem to say the right things in interviews. Some people are trained or are experienced in a given field and are unwilling to ring registers, drive fork lifts or pack out while their own work gets kicked to the curb. If you have to do everything how can you be expected to do your own job well? Yes at retail you need to step up when needed but when that need becomes part of a daily routine there is something wrong going on.

THE TOP BANANA

I do agree that rotating people between club and home office would improve empathy, problem solving and problem avoidence.

I have seen overnight managers work 7 days straight and/or 10 plus hours per day. Having this happen is poor management and sets the bar to high as a standard to meet. Some of these managers I've seen go through this actually think this will endear them to club management only to find they are hating their job, expect others to admire or feel bad for them; then they get passed over for a day shift position by an outside hire or a transfer. Work smarter and not harder isn't just a saying it's effective. Managers should plan, execute and review not grind themselves into the concrete floor.

This passage came from a book excerpt from one of the bloggers.

A few demeaning creeps can overwhelm the warm feelings generated by hordes of civilized people.

The abuse spewed out by just one jerk was ruining the experience for everyone at Little Joe's that day. Remember that if you want to enforce the no-asshole rule in your organization, you'll get more bang for your buck by eliminating those folks who bring people down. Bear in mind that negative interactions have five times the effect on mood as positive interactions -- it takes a lot of good people to make up for the damage done by just a few demeaning jerks. If you want a civilized workplace, take some inspiration from the CEO who made up the equivalent of 25 "asshole wanted" posters and then purged those assholes from the company. So the first things that you need to do are screen out, reform and expel all the assholes in

THE TOP BANANA

your workplace. It will then become easier to focus on helping people become warmer and more supportive.

Talking about or posting the rule isn't necessary if people understand it and act on it. But if you can't enforce the rule, it is better to say nothing. Otherwise, your organization risks being seen as both nasty and hypocritical. Recall the fate of Holland & Knight, the law firm that bragged it had "made it a priority to weed out selfish, arrogant and disrespectful attorneys" and that it would enforce a "no-jerk rule." It faced bad press when insiders expressed disgust with the firm's hypocrisy because an attorney with an alleged history of sexual harassment was promoted to a senior management position.

Talking about the rule is nice, but following up on it is what really matters.
The incident at Little Joe's shows that very bad people can be a very good thing -- if they are handled right. That flaming asshole was perfect for Chapter 13 because his antics showed every customer and employee in that crowded place how not to behave at that place. But I want to warn you that allowing a few creeps to make themselves at home in your company is dangerous. The truth is that assholes breed like rabbits. Their poison quickly infects others; even worse, if you let them make hiring decisions, they will start cloning themselves. Once people believe that they can get away with treating others with contempt or, worse yet, believe they will be praised and rewarded for it, a reign of psychological terror can spread throughout your organization that is damn hard to stop.

Enforcing the no-asshole rule isn't just management's job.[1]

Chapter Two: The Monkey Method

I wish I had permission to use the picture of one particular chimp from the Career Builder commercials that aired during SuperBowl XL. It was the boss chimp in the pinstripe suit that was smoking a cigar, burning some cash, and was proud that sales were up. Then the human in the meeting told everyone sales weren't up, they were down, and turned the sales chart right-side up. This caused a moment of temporary shock and disbelief before one rank-and-file chimp changed the chart back to the way it was, allowing the big party to resume. The boss made a gesture, and the human joined the party and became just another dancing monkey.

BJ's has seemed to survive the holidays and reports that sales are up. Meanwhile at their Danvers location certain potentially discriminatory practices are taking place

*BJ'S has had MANY locations with practices that DO NOT follow company policy and procedure AND
practices that border on violating
state and federal law.*

1.Using the classification game to skirt the overtime issue for managers

THE MONKEY METHOD

While most SENIOR managers are exempt from FLSA overtime regulations, the rest of the management team IS NOT

2. Sexual Harassment Issues
Straight and Gay

3. Misleading injured workers about Workers Compensation

4. Wrongful Termination

According to federal guidelines, the work you actually do, not the job title determines exemption. Overnight managers stock shelves, drive fork lifts, reset sections and spend very little to no time actually managing. Recently, Corporate HR told store managers to have a day manager in by 7am, this never happens. So now you are "Volunteering to Stay" in current BJ"S lingo.

This was another poster's reply.

"Didn't Personnel Managers get settlement for this a few years back? Maybe Overnight Managers need to investigate the specifics of the FLSA regualtions"?? Unknown to that person, one Overnight Manager already had. [3]

RE: WORKERS COMPENSATION
They are self insured, and actually have charts that claim a charge out for a lost work day claim is $26,000, charge out for a medical claim is $6,000. They like to keep this quiet because bad publicity is an indirect cost, and bad publicity reduces profits and ultimately sales, and regulatory violations and fines. Ask to see page 8 of the New Club Management Orientation

THE MONKEY METHOD

handout, dealing with safety and sanitation. They like to play hardball, especially with workers comp cases; when I was injured on the job, I had to threaten to sue them to get me to see a specialist; their doctor said it was a contusion, the specialist said I had to learn to live with it, that arthritis and tendinitis would develop, but that there would be no true grounds for a suit because range of motion was not totally lost; the cost to sue would be more than a potential settlement.

RE: SEXUAL HARASSMENT
Straight Issues:
Senior Managers Harassing Mids
& Hourlies
Mids Harassing Mids & Hourlies
Hourlies Harassing Hourlies

Gay Issues:
A lesbian showing pictures of her and her significant other in various acts in an attempt to have straight single or married woman JOIN IN with them. When this was brought to the attention of a SENIOR who is a lesbian, her comment was " Are you sure they are targeting her because of her appearance ". Company policy DICTATES that this behavior goes to IMMEDIATE FINAL WRITE UP, no questions asked. The senior had real issues with the IMMEDIATE FINAL WRITE UP, so her hand was forced when the victim CALLED CORPORATE and explained the situation. The employee had done the picture trick to others, so she was IMMEDIATELY terminated, and the Senior took offense to that action

DESPITE it being in the company handbook.
About a year later, it appears that same senior manager was still conducting business as usual, based on this post. "I know

THE MONKEY METHOD

an OPS that doctored paperwork, and all the GM cared about was passing audits....this same OPS, driving a forklift, ripped steel from the floor.... this same OPS, when confronted with a sexual harassment issue, tried to pass off the incident as " perhaps people do not like her appearance "... this lesbian employee was trying to get other females to " join in " with her and her partner, and had pictures showing their behavior..... this same OPS NEVER worked overnights, yet got to the OPS position... Wonder what she had on somebody....."

RE: TERMINATION
Most employees in the United States are at-will employees, even though most employees are unaware of this situation. In most states, the law presumes that private sector employees are employed "at-will." The employment-at-will doctrine provides that both the employer and the employee can end the employment relationship at any time without notice or reason. This means the employer has the right to terminate your employment at any time, for any reason, or for no reason at all or for a bad reason, so long as the reason is not illegal - even if you performance has been outstanding.

MANY good employees (Hourlies and Management) have been terminated because someone had "an issue" with them. Because of this law, BJ'S does win most of the cases; but they have also lost a few.

Before you find yourself in this position, DOCUMENT everything and trust NO ONE at store or DM position. Send it right to corporate.

Chapter Three: Monkey Ways of Thinking

"Can you clock me in? I need an override", the Asset Protection (AP) Clerical team member asked the Overnight Food Specialist. Before I go into the rest of interaction, I want to disclose that the AP Clerical was once a Front Line Supervisor who was promoted to Customer Service Manager (CSM) when the CSM at the time went on leave for medical reasons. When the CSM felt better, she returned, and her replacement was promptly demoted. This happens often at BJ's. No matter how well you may perform as a temporary manager, even if it exceeds the performance of the incumbent manager, once the incumbent returns, you get demoted. No GM or Regional Manager (RM) is going to help you keep your new position, or recommend options for you to keep your status.

While on the topic of promotions, it is mind boggling how power ebbs and flows at BJs. One Overnight Food Specialist told me the guy coming back from short term disability to work in the dairy, used to be his overnight specialist when he started with the company. The favortism he showed his former boss was astonishing! He could come in, and start talking to his new boss for numerous minutes before doing any work. The demigods liked him, and so did the Gods of Mount Olympus. He looked like a male model and was built like Hercules. When the dairy guy got promoted to Deli Manager, I took over for him. By the way, I helped persuade him that it was a good move that could lead him back to being an overnight specialist making a lot more money because of the shift differential and overtime. Initially, he didn't want the promotion because he didn't like the starting salary when compared to the money he made as an overnight specialist. I didn't get that special treatment in the dairy. In fact, when I would come in early to get ahead, the Overnight Food Specialist would ambush me before I went to the dairy, and have me help his side out when he was short staffed. He always overworked any good guys he had. Never once did he ask his former boss to do that. My mental health took a plunge, I had anxiety attacks, and had to go to a doctor for medication. Later, his mental health took a plunge, and he lost it right in front of a freezer team member and the same GM who promoted him to overnight specialist. He went on short term disability, and while on it, had a vehicle accident. When he returned to work, he came back in a very low level position-recovery clerk. Then he went to the deli where he cried to the GM who was like a mother to him. She got him out of the dairy and put him on overnight. Later, there were some management transfers, and she gave him his something he wanted for a while-a salaried daytime management position. As Receiving and Inventory Control Manager [RICM], he and his former boss were equals! But some time later, in January 2016, he was told he would be out of a job because BJ's was phasing out certain positions and consolidating others. His former boss, the Deli Manager, learned that unless deli sales met or exceeded a certain amount each week, his position would change from salaried manager to hourly supervisor with much lower pay and authority. Once again, the Gods smiled upon him, transferred one overnight specialist, and gave him an

MONKEY WAYS OF THINKING

Overnight Replishment Specialist position. Later, he too stepped down from stress.

As a mid manager, you are over anyone who is not your superior. It means much more responsibility, but with that comes special privileges, a generous raise to being on salary, and bonuses. The position was never listed as Temporary CSM, so we all felt badly for her. But when the CSM suddenly got transferred back to her original club, she got her new position back, one she excelled at doing. Later, something happened that nobody saw coming...except upper management. January 2016, there was a mass purge of management positions and other salaried positions, from the Home Office level to the club level in a failed effort to trim the fat and get rid of redundancy, dead wood, and managers who'd been with the company "too long", meaning they made too much. This was worse than the club closings in 2011.[4]

She was demoted again, this time to Receiving & Inventory Control Supervisor (RICS). The RICM was given a severance package, and shown the door. Being a trooper, she took the demotion well. Then another blow hit, in the form of the RM almost totally cleaning house and installing his own regime of soldiers. Next thing she knew, she was demoted yet again! With each demotion, she lost status and pay. New management didn't think she was doing a good enough job, so it demoted her. Being the person she was, she took the demotion and did not fight the pay decrease. Fortunately, friends of hers told her to fight it because she didn't choose the demotion. She stated her case, fought it, and won!

Once in possession of keys and numbers [override codes, alarm codes], as an hourly non-manager, she was now at the

MONKEY WAYS OF THINKING

mercy of those who would have been her peers.
"Am I going to get yelled at?, he asked her, "I don't want to get yelled at again". "____ told me last night that it was OK. He sent me a text. You want to see it"? Proof is something managers or specialists rarely want to see. It is a form of kryptonite to them. "You have ____ fix it with HR. The last time I gave someone an override to start early, I got yelled at."

Once upon a time, managers and specialists had override cards to override hourly employees who had electronic swipe cards used to clock themselves in and out. Override cards were anonymous striped cards, not tied to anyone, which they could use to clock hourly employees in early, on a day off, or if they arrived late for their shift. Or to clock them out, if they stayed past their scheduled time. Overrides are supposed to only be used for legitimate reasons. Unlike the former NonFood Manager who got suspended and fired for using his card to swipe his girlfriend in for work when she was nowhere near the building.

When an hourly team member comes in early, it is for a reason. No employee loves their job so much, they lie in bed, then suddenly have the urge to wake up much earlier than their scheduled shift, and want to come to work! This is especially true if they have an early morning shift, say 5 AM-1 PM. Override cards went away, and were replaced with employee ID numbers and punching them into the clock. No longer anonymous, managers and specialists had to give reason for every override, and that made them nervous. If an override looked questionable, they had to account for it. So now employees receive a police inquisition whenever they show up early for work or on their day off.

MONKEY WAYS OF THINKING

But these are the ones in charge, the ones in power, the bosses, the leaders. I honestly think going into mid management and senior management at BJ's dumbs otherwise intelligent people down. When they were hourly or in supervisor positions, they were much sharper. But as managers and specialists, they are merely puppets who are told what to do by those higher up in the food chain than they are. It is a domino effect of dumbness. Let us see what the BJ's bloggers say about it.

*It's the same with mid managers becoming senior managers. Even if they are willing to do their overnight "prison sentence", the time it takes to be promoted is discouraging. They keep the dead weight senior managers around and keep the mid managers that could make positive changes in limbo. Hopefully **Rf** sees the whole picture and not only make changes with GMs, but with senior management staff as well.*

*Why is it that managers who have been with the company for many many yrs have to jump threw hoops to be promoted to senior management. They have to be tortured with the whole overnight experience to be promoted to a senior. Then **J B** hires his brother as a Senior Merchant from outside the company. Someone who has NO RETAIL EXPERIENCE, didn't have to make his way through the ranks of Mid to overnight to senior mamanger. And I'm sure he wasn't hired at a starting Senior Management pay rate. So when the corupt policies and procedures come from someone as high up as Jay Breslin, how can you expect club level managers to follow policy?????*

MONKEY WAYS OF THINKING

The same thing happens in NJ. How did an employee get to OPS without working overnights. She was SOOO incompetent that she almost caused a disaster with a forklift. I did what I had to do to stop the disaster, and yet she is still with the company.

I can beat that, Im working in a club who is trainning a Senior Manager. This guy is required not to work any overnites. The best part about this guy is he has quit Bj's twice, and has come back. So to reward him for quiting the company we are going to make him a senior manager and he isnt required to put in the guidelines of being promoted to a senior as the rest of us are. Thats Discrimination. Thats how this regional works. If she likes you, your in. If she doesnt you will never be promoted.

J's brother works in 153 and he started as a mid (LP) not a senior. Not that i like him he doesnt know what hes doing hes an AWFUL OPS.

LP to OPS with no overnights. Nepotism at its finest

Can **M B** come back to club 13 now? Most still really miss her! She was one that would jump in and help out from ringing register to mopping floors when the FLS's couldn't get to it due to lines. No matter how many times she was paged, she answered everyone. She never made you feel stupid for asking questions and although she had her bad days, even then she was still nicer then some of the other managers. She asked us to do jobs instead of ordering us. If we needed to push carts in the raind or snow, she was right there besides us. She used the words please and thank you. I really hope the powers that be are smart enough not to waste her on the overnight shift vrey long. And if she doesn't come back to club 13, her next club is

MONKEY WAYS OF THINKING

extremly lucky to get her! **M B** we miss you - come home soon!

As mentioned before, the ONLY way she can become a SENIOR is to do her overnight prison sentence at Hamilton. She WAS the BEST Manager remaining at 13.
one thing i could not stand working at bj's the day crew and managers did nothing to help out on the floor they would walk in at 7am stand around talk drink their coffee ..unless it was a day of a home office visit you never seen people move around soooo fast like chickens with their heads cut off ..begging people on the overnight crew to stay (always find magic money) overnight crew pretty much telling them to get bent after being treated like crap every other day ..we had a receiving dept whos last truck came in at 8 am the rest of the day just sat in the back of the store making free money...and god forbid if you asked the receiving manager to have the receivers help out on the floor

Hey, here's a crazy idea. Ship **Ca** back to Hamilton and bring back **M B** to Maple Shade. She is truely missed by a ton of us employees!!

When I was a mid with the company, I was asked to train a person in the GMIT program. This guy came from the outside, and had NO CLUE what was going on. Imagine that, I got to train a future boss. He had a very poor work ethic and felt he was better than everybody else. He did not last too long with the company. Yet those who do what is requested of them get denied promotional opportunities all the time.

hmm.. I think I know the manager you are talking about... training in 100 maybe? well from what little I heard... he left

MONKEY WAYS OF THINKING

because of one of those bad seed managers that we all love talking about on here, and the story I heard was pretty bad... anyone in their right mind would have left... so who knows maybe he did do his time... I'm not saying the must do the overnights thing is right by any strech, I think it should be done away with... it means nothing, so many good people get passed over because they can't do overnights, not because they don't want to or won't... some of us have children, and can't leave them at night... it's sad. I hope they see that, and change the rule. Hate on the people who make the stupid rules..
besides... I think the Jay's brother thing is way worse!

What the hell was **Rf** thinking by changing GM's right before inventory. That was not to brite on his part.and bringing a GM that isn't even wet behind the ears.He is from a low volume club like Deptford,And how about all the people getting fired for stealing,and yes that was under **Mk's** Management in Deptford.Yeah transfer him to a high volume club that's the answer.Now **Ri** has to deal with the mess and have to fill all those positions.The next thing you'll here is that **Mk** became a regional some where,that's what happens with this company when you screw up you move up.Or if your a manger kiss up,and that a damm shame if you have to be that way,with your regionals or the VP.

An operations manager just got screwed in the linden club, it goes to show that no matter what you do you aint safe. This guy really changed club 67 around and he got the shaft for allegedly giving out his alarm codes but it was all payback from his gm since he tried to get her for a scheme she had going if I were him I would sue BJ's for discrimination he had all the evidence

MONKEY WAYS OF THINKING

and she didnt get fired because she knows someone in the Home Office totally BS

Our DM paid a visit to our club this morning, with nothing nice to say. She goes out of her way to point out elementary schisms. She always seems to attack our dept. Maybe it's because we have a female-male imbalance. She rides in on her high horse, while claiming she's a vegetarian, but she's easily over 260 lbs. What kind of vegatarian is overweight?

i think that the company is a huge joke. the managers sit there like they are god and rein over all of the little pee-ons. while the little pee-ons are down there watching and scheming on how to make their managers life a living hell... and no one sees that this is going on. they cant give you anything that they promise. they cant keep a deal to save their pethatic little lives and they have NO respect for the people who make the company possible (all the little employees ex: anyone who is NOT a manager). maybe you should try showing your employees that you actually give a damn about them and the company would run a whole lot smoother and have a much higher success rate... just something to think about for all you so called "managers". sad part is i dont even work for the company, i am just a frequent shopper and can see all of this stuff happening. you make your employees miserble, which in retutrn makes us, the customers miserble!

since when does bjs become aplace where nobody cares how can two inviduals be allowed to carry out a dictatorship kind of rule and nothing is done.since when does bjs hire people from outside into senior level positions and team members that has given teir sacrafice to this company for a number of years be

MONKEY WAYS OF THINKING

overlooked spme times positions are not even posted.promote individuls om merit and knowlege not by friends and the colr of their skin.

*its been along time since i had to work a thanksgiving night and this year is no different tell **Rf** that he should show up with the other managers at 4 am and please bring along a pair of jeans and gloves the overnight managers is going to need your help CASTRO.*

Favoritism is at ALL clubs.
Managers disliking each other is at all clubs.
Stupid write ups occur at all clubs.
Threats occur at all clubs.
As long as the club is running and doing OK, an investigation will NEVER occur.

I manager, I no education to be one but still I manager, I ask how high when told to jump, I think of I, I learn from other I managers. I never plan, I do. BJ's suffers from stone age management. I never wrong, I always right.
You hourly, you work for me, you bite tongue when I think of me. If I wrong I don't admit I put you in place. I panic when you have good idea, I break company policy, no one care as long as I do. You almost manager, but I manager and I can do and say what ever I want to you but I use bobblehead technique with my Sr. manager therefore I rule. I treat you like shit because I have power and you don't. You too stupid to get union to check my power. I call you piece of shit behind your back, I manager I better than you. Life sucks for you, it sucks for me too.
I am not proud of being manager at BJ's I just need the cash.

MONKEY WAYS OF THINKING

What is the company that we work for thinking about...how the hell are they going to open another new club? They should focus on the ones that they already have open, the sucky ones really need some special attention! Take some of that extra money that you guys are spending on a new club and divide between the ones that you already have! More payroll = happy team members = equals happy MEMBERS!! Just do the equation, simple math is not that difficult...It didn't take a Home Office genious to figure out, I'm just a cashier!

Costco's productivity is far greater than BJ's Wholesale Club will ever be, thanks in part to undereducated management.

The clubs in our region tend to be underachieving. We have two very profitible clubs, with the rest of the region being a mess to say the least.

The perishible departents contribute greatly to a club's success. Our club has been underachieving since the day it opened, and we have zero "wholesale" competion. We are the only wholesale club in the entire county, and we can't put up the numbers that we could be doing. With passive management, this is what happens. A lazy meat manager who comes and goes as he pleases, while a business member's request go unfulfilled. Our produce department tends to leave spoiled product out on the sales floor, which leaves a bad impression to all of the members.

Bj's should stick to the basics, listen to your members and employ competent team members and management.
Hello TM, I don't work overnight but I do respect n know how much they have to do at night. They have to restock the store

MONKEY WAYS OF THINKING

with very little help. When the manager comes in the morning they don't let them leave on time, they r already tried from work they do at night. It's just basically sad that seeing hard working tm n managers get mess with or fired n the other lazy managers don't do nothing n don't know what they are doing, they get away with lots of things cuz they know how to kiss ass and the upper level likes them. They need to open their eyes and see who is actually working or pretending to work n don't know what they are doing.I do respect all of the TM and Managers who work hard for their money.I know they don't get appreciate for the hard work cuz when u have a bad store manager or senior managers. They only worried for themselves, thats not teamwork that is call selfish. I only talking about the lazy TM n Managers. The only thing I want to say is I respect all hard working TM n Manager. I hope that the upper level see that and don't mess with those TM n Manager.

Here's a good question. How does someone who doesn't apply for an FLS position, and doesn't want an FLS position get one? Meanwhile there are other people who actually take the time to fill out the application and are looking for advancement in the company. They won't ever get interviewed. And once again, management won't care. They are at fault. So instead of giving the promotion to someone who might actually deserve it, we will give it to someone with a bad attitude who thinks that they are too pretty to do any real work. And also happens to have an "in" in the company. You be the judge.

And as far as the new LP manager goes, good for **Ang!** I think she deserves it. I don't know that she was the most qualified and she doesn't have the most seniority, but **Ri** and **Mch** had to pick who they thought was best to handle the job. **Ang** knows

MONKEY WAYS OF THINKING

what it is like being on the side of the little people. Hopefully she will just remember the hard times and where she came from. And she is hardly the type that sits around chatting like other managers.

I made this former comment before...
"What corporate should do is contact former employees (hourlies and management) to find out the what REALLY happens at the clubs".
I AM STILL WAITING FOR A WAY TO CONTACT L, OR TO HAVE HER CONTACT ME !!!!!!

What is why **Rf** is at # 13 today (5-14-09)and EVERYBODY is scrambling around like chickens with their head cut off.

Ad was a liar, promising everything and delivering nothing.

BJ'S has lost MANY more "extremely good" people (hourly & management) than "bad eggs". Most (NOT ALL) of the management that are left are "heartless villains ", doing just enough to keep their jobs. Corporate has NO idea what is happening, all they are concerned with is the bottom line, which effects the hourlies more than the management. Many problems get hidden from corporate, thus they
(Corporate) have NO IDEA what is going on. Should that surprise you?

I could compose for hours about the
incidents I witnessed at many of the Clubs I worked or helped out at. Company policy and procedure was tossed out the window and it was business as usual with a don't tell policy. What corporate should do is contact former employees

MONKEY WAYS OF THINKING

(hourlies and management) to find out the what REALLY happens at the clubs.

i dunno if managers don't know how to manage or if they are afraid to..when i was a manager there any ideas i had for product placement was met with a scared look on their faces and a "will have to get it approved from home office" answer(yes god forbid i add some extra coke pallets on the floor for the holidays)..all the stores have to look alike(don't ask me why) different areas sell different products at different rates yet they all have to look alike ..i guess if someone from maine is traveling to iowa they will know right where their jar of pickles are..hey but keep up the good work bj's your making everyone that works there miserable good plan!!nothing like an unhappy worker

Interesting analogy...
Comparing the theory of sum zero with unions, believing that unions would make it a win-win for all.

We all know about Walmart. Unions have tried and failed numerous times to enter the doors of the worlds Largest Retailer in the USA.

We all know about Costco. Select former Price Club stores (purchased by Costco) are run by the Teamsters. Guess what.... Costco management treats non-union employees like the union employees in California.

What BJ'S SHOULD do is follow the lead of Costco, who is #1 in the membership warehouse club business and the #3 retailer in the USA, by

MONKEY WAYS OF THINKING

utilizing their policy and procedures to obtain a content and productive workforce.

If the number 1 and 3 retailers in the USA can do it without unions, why should a chain of 180 stores (BJ'S) even entertain the idea of unions.

Latona *YAY club 1310/07/2008 5:52 AM*
I work at club #13 in Maple Shade and I would like to take this opportunity to say something. I know that everyone reads this blog so maybe now I can get their attention, more so than I do at work. In my opinion, everyone's attitude at our club needs to change. When I say everyone, it includes mine. I have been working here for 5 years now, and each day, I get more disgruntled. I would like my job more if I felt a little more appreciated. I do not want to point fingers or call out names, all I want is to suggest the following.

#1 let's help out each other more. FLSs, let's help out the membership desk when the lines get long. membership desk, let's try not to get upset when asked to ring, but the other side to that is, if there are 3 FLSs standing around and wants us to jump on because they don't want to ring, that isn't fair. I can't speak for everyone, but I know that I volunteer to ring register a lot. On top of that, I do box bins, assist members on the floor, run jewelry, watch the front, and many other tasks. I put in a lot and I just want some of that reciprocated. Cashier's, some of you guys just don't care, and members can tell. I know some of you guys don't want to really work, but you are at work anyway, so make the best out of it.

#2 managers-some of you guys are 80 levels of awesomeness

MONKEY WAYS OF THINKING

and I love out. I actually like all of the managers. Each one has their own distinguishing feature that makes them who they are. with that being said, some managers are less willing to help out when the lines at membership get long or even when the front line has a question. then when something goes wrong, that is our problem and then we are in trouble. No one should feel afraid to ask for help. So, although the front line needs to change in order to bring up the morale of the club, so do the managers. I know it is difficult to worry about getting your own work done and helping out other people, but isn't that what being a manager is all about. like I said, I am not finger pointing, but let's all look at ourselves and see where our attitudes can improve.

#3- PLEASE AND THANK YOU

these words are so simple and I use them all of the time. Some cashiers blink their lights and just stare at you as if you should be a mind reader. Then, some of them just hand you a reshop, not informing you whether or not there is something wrong with it until you have fish juice all over you or until the milk leaks all over the floor. communication is simple and we are listening. Oh and by the way-please and thank you. And that is not just for cashiers. Little words say big things.

#4 Politeness

Some people are very rude and do not realize it. When you ask them politely for something, they throw it down on the counter and walk off as if you have interrupted their hard work. Maybe so, but don't we all do hard work? It isn't easy working the long lines of the service desk ALONE. It isn't easy running the front

MONKEY WAYS OF THINKING

line ALONE. So let's put on our happy faces and act like we enjoy helping each other.

#5 Managers Recourse

There are employees that I know must bug the pants off of the managers, because they bug me too. It is difficult to WANT to be helpful when there is so much bad attitude in the air. People are working when they want to work, taking extra long breaks just because they can get away with it, and they are acting like you owe them something because YOU need them. Newsflash---We are all expendable. That includes me. So get over yourselves and put on those happy faces. You get further with smiles than you do with frowns.

#6 The bottom line

The best thing we can do is to make each other feel appreciated. If we don't bring each other up, all the good guys who have been sweet, kind, and helpful will GO TO THE DARKSIDE. I am staring to turn. So, I will start by naming one peron I appreciated. And instead of bashing people, i hope I can start a chain of who we appreciate in our club and why.

I appreciate **Cyn** for being our MARM. Some people apparently don' think she works hard enough, but I see first hand all that she does. It isn't having to do her own work, covering the service desk(b/c we are understaffed but not for long thank goodness), covering the front line, and trying to satisfy the members. Many of the members love her, because she actually listens to them. Some don't like her because she likes to follow the rules. Whatever the case, walk a day in her shoes. At least

MONKEY WAYS OF THINKING

she is smiling everyday.

Yours truly, because I love all of you and hate that I can cut the air with a knife,

Latona club 13

Before you all go jumping on the Costco bandwagon, read this about Costco and tell me if it sounds familiar.....

"The culture that I and my colleagues have experienced is one of micro-management by intimidation. I have worked with a couple of general managers and dozens of area managers and I have found that with regard to hourly employees' behavior, they unanimously assume negative intent. Simply implementing #13 on your list of things you believe would alone make a marked difference in this environment. When instructions are given about completing a task, these instructions are always coupled with a criticism. Employees are often told to be team players but management doesn't exhibit a team attitude themselves. I have endless examples of this but I don't want to lose you now, if I haven't already. I know you must get endless emails.

So how might any of this affect the bottom line? I have noticed a trend over the years that I've been with Costco of employees demoting themselves. I have personally known of 6 individuals who have taken up to a 15,000/year pay cut to "step down." In some cases the other management at the store described this self demotion as a "personal failure on the part of the employee." I have not experienced these individuals to be

MONKEY WAYS OF THINKING

failures and some of them are the most intelligent and productive workers that I have had the pleasure of working with, and they are also Nice! On the flip side of this, managers that have had numerous complaints made about their behavior are continuing to get promoted. One such individual had no less than 10 people about his unprofessional, condescending, and almost downright abusive behavior. Upper management's response was that they would speak to him, but that he will continue on in his current role.

Finally, it's important to note that I'm not basing this on only my experience or on the experiences at one location. I've networked with Costco employees in Seattle, Florida and Indiana to name a few and I have found similar environments and similar stories. So why am I still here? Why are some of my colleagues still here? The pay and the benefits no doubt play a part, but so has the idea that we can change things".

The grass is NOT always greener

Chapter Four: Bachelor Degree in Monkey Business

It is usually a given there is a title for the next position attained in a promotion. Supervisors, Leads, and Shift Leaders become Assistant Managers, and later, GM's...hopefully. Based upon the industry, District Managers or Regional Managers who are Assistant Vice Presidents become Vice Presidents, then Senior Vice Presidents, then Executive Vice Presidents, and then Senior Executive Vice Presidents. There are Directors, Managing Directors, Partners, Senior Partners, etc. The list is almost never ending based on how the company titles its positions in hierarchy. But sometimes, there is no next higher position. So somebody up high "creates" one for a crony, golf buddy, frat brother, sorority sister, or relative.

BJ's Wholesale Club Inc. announced Thursday that **Edward F. Gillooly** *was promoted to the newly created position of executive vice president, chief marketing officer.*
Gillooly had been senior vice president, director of marketing.
Gillooly, whose career at BJ's began in 1991, brings more than 20 years of marketing experience to his new position.
He began at BJ's as assistant vice president, marketing director. A year later he was promoted to vice president in that

BACHELOR DEGREE IN MONKEY BUSINESS

department. He was promoted again, but retired in September 2002. He returned to BJ's in January 2007 to lead the marketing department.[1]

Would you believe, you don't need any in depth or academic training to become a manager at BJ's? They state "college graduate preferred" on internal job postings, but it's not needed. At BJ's, senior management and mid management readily switch from one role to another. One week, you could be Senior Merchant, the next week, you are Operations Manager. One week, you could be CSM or MSM, the next week, Loss Prevention Manager [LPM], which was renamed Asset Protection Manager (APM), and is now Asset Control Manager (ACM). Mind you, unless it is a promotion, it is just a lateral move. You are given a crash course on the new position, and then you are on your own. The good thing about BJ's is as a manager or specialist, unless you do something very, very wrong, or very, very stupid, you can be there forever.

Here is a quote from Brian Krzanich, the CEO of Intel Corp., the world's largest maker of computer chips. He was just an engineer when he made a mistake that almost got him fired. The mistake made its way all the way to the CEO at the time, which led to his boss giving him an ultimatum. Krzanich and a friend resolved the problem, which saved his job. He shared this advice with his daughters, "The other thing I tell my daughters is, I've had to terminate or fire more people for being difficult to work with than being dumb."[8]

One historic example of doing something very, very stupid, was the story about the GM who had an employee stand on the bare forks of his standing forklift, and lifted him all the way to the

BACHELOR DEGREE IN MONKEY BUSINESS

ceiling to do something. The procedure is to place a cage on the forks, chain the cage to the mast of the forklift, and the employee(s) in the cage have to wear a hardhat. It just so happened that during this fantastic demonstration of stupidity, the Regional Loss Prevention Manager [renamed Regional Asset Protection Manager from RLPM to RAPM] was there. He saw all he needed, made a call to the Regional Manager, and that was the end of the GM's career with BJ's. A common phrase at BJ's is "We don't fire people at BJ's; people fire themselves".

Consider what a recently retired employee from the Pennsylvania Turnpike Commission said in a company-wide sent email.[1] There is monkey business in the public and private sector.

Asked in the questionnaire what the most upsetting part of the job was, Stuban unloaded.

"The phoneyness," he wrote.

"Giving us classes where we are being told we are not political," he wrote. "That's bulls---. Jobs/Promotions are filled by the politicians, it's who you know, not what you know. Positions created for people who are not qualified. Hiring people off the street when we have qualified [personnel] in our ranks."

Stuban also claimed that commission employees "have no morale" and that executive-level management is "out of touch with the average employees" and "only looking out for themselves."

BACHELOR DEGREE IN MONKEY BUSINESS

"He did miss the point," Stuban said. "If it was an effective company and someone told you there are problems and no morale, you don't have to believe me, but maybe someone should check into it."

"They hire a lot of people that are dumb as rocks," he added.

Of course, when it reached the excutive level, that is, the Chairman of the Turnpike Commission, he was predictably rattled by this, and gave a predictable set of replies.

The message was not well received by Sean Logan, chairman of the Turnpike Commission. Logan, a former Pennsylvania state senator, decided to fire back at the outgoing employee and also hit the reply-all button, writing: "Mr. Stuban .?.?. I don't believe we ever met, and after reading your Exit Questionnaire, I am grateful that we didn't."

Retaliation. This is the primary reason employees do not voice or pen their true thoughts and feelings to their bosses. Even those in middle and upper middle management, remain silent to senior and executive management for fear of retaliation. Have you ever seen television shows or movies where the messenger delivered bad news to a ruler with much trepidation? Sometimes it resulted in immediate death. How about the one dissident to a ruler's way to doing things that were beneficial to those in power, but not the people? Same fate-death.

Logan told PennLive that the message was the first time he'd been made aware of Stuban's frustration and said he didn't appreciate the means of delivery.

BACHELOR DEGREE IN MONKEY BUSINESS

Just as The Architect told Neo in "The Matrix", denial is the most predictable human response.

"I thought it was a very disingenuous way to communicate your issues," Logan said. *"If he really wanted to be constructive with his criticisms and suggestions, there's a whole other way to do it."*

Right.

I saw a YouTube video featuring businessman, author, and motivational speaker, Brian Tracy. He mentioned that areas of the government purposely do not want to solve problems because if they did, they would no longer have jobs. In the 1957 movie, "12 Angry Men", the jurors were genuinely passionate about the assigned case. But now, it is about seeing how long can a person can stay away from the job, away from her husband, away from his wife, or boring life.

Quite a lot of managers step down after they can no longer take the stupidity and stress. The one group of management known to actually walk out on the job are Overnight Specialists. That is considered job abandonment in most realities. But at BJ's, its reality has a double standard. If a non-manager or non-specialist team member walks out on the job, nobody calls them to find out what happened, and what can be done to get them to come back. That only applies to managers and specialists. Why? Are they better than regular team members? Certainly not. Many of them once were regular team members. But managers and specialists take more time to replace. It wreaks havoc on the remaining one who have to carry the extra

BACHELOR DEGREE IN MONKEY BUSINESS

workload. So their bosses scramble to coddle them, and get them to continue working until they can find a replacement. The funny thing is, it's always some of the biggest in size, or toughest in attitude who fold, turn in their keys, and walk out the door. It's never small guys or women.

Another wild reality is BJ's backward mentality about the weak and the strong. Anyone familiar with herd mentality knows just as the animal kingdom does, the strong survive, and the weak are weeded out through natural causes, or eaten. Not at BJ's. The strong are the ones with the bullseye on the back, and the weak are left alone to flourish, like weeds in a yard. I remember once, when I was a cashier, someone in management thought we were overstaffed. Just like when there are more jurors available than needed, managers began sending people home. But unlike at the courthouse, where the first ones to the counter to get waivers gets to leave, management handpicked who went home. Guess who got to rest if they had a second job to go to later, enjoy the rest of the day, or go spend time with their families? You guessed it, the bench warmers. They kept all the starters on the registers, and let the members burn them out for eight hours. The strong need more of a break than the weak by the simple fact that they work harder. Did you know Larry Bird ran miles before and after his games? Even though his team practice had two hour runs, he still felt that wasn't enough.[7] Every department has team members whose individual efforts are worth the efforts of 2-3 lazy team members. And it is those team members who get "dish ragged" while the others stay clean.

I always say, "just because they are managers, doesn't make them smart". It doesn't make them any better than those who

BACHELOR DEGREE IN MONKEY BUSINESS

work under them either. A friend of mine got promoted to Temporary Overnight Non-Food Specialist. He got a big raise, had keys and numbers, and the coveted gold badge. I have such wonderful metaphors for their gold badges, which I will get into later.

My friend was as good as I was because I trained him. After he got additional, personal training under the wing of our Senior Merchant, I admit, he became better than me. My problem was I worked hard; he worked smart. My senior merchant wanted to promote me to Overnight Supervisor. I recommended my friend because he needed it more. He had a wife, daughter, vehicle, and house. He got the position, and when the temporary position came, I encouraged him to apply for it. It was natural for him. He did far better than the guy he replaced. He got all his work done on time, his floor was clear early, all of his folks left on time, and he never had overtime. The bad thing was, he became a jerk to all of us, including me. I felt like Obi-Wan Kenobi looking at Anakin once he went to the Dark Side. He was Nicaraguan, and was like a brother to me. My Overnight Specialist friend before him was Cuban. We were like brothers too. That was until he started monkeying around with a girl who transferred there from the Zone Vice President's club farther up north. She was the beginning of his end. You will read about her later.

The floor fell from under my friend when the guy who he replaced returned to work. You'd think they would've fought to keep my friend in that position, and transfer the incumbent. But this is BJ's. Just as at the Home Office and upper management levels, senior management doesn't alway make the best decisions. He was promptly demoted, and none of us wanted to

BACHELOR DEGREE IN MONKEY BUSINESS

be around him. I did my best to get things back the way they were between us because just as Darth Vader did, he came back to the Light Side of the Force.

He had a second job, which luckily he didn't quit. I guess he saw it coming. But none of us saw his personality change coming. I honestly don't think he did either.

Let's see what the bloggers think about management promotions.

It is amazing who gets promoted to Management. While they may have been decent as a Cashier, FLS or in Member Services, they have NO IDEA that they must act like professional adults as management. Too bad most of them DO NOT UNDERSTAND THAT.

I just have a quick question. Is there any particular reason why Club 013 is getting all Shoprites reject managers? I mean, **Ri** *wasn't the greatest manager of all time, but they decide to replace him with a GM that got canned from Shoprite. A GM by the way who really enjoys sitting in his office all day every day and watching his worker ants through his darkened windows. I just don't get it. Probably never will...*

Greetings from #109 again!

OK, its official. As of this week, we have a new RICM, moved from a sister club farther south. So now that club needs one, unless a mid-manager moved there from another club. Its been about a month, or so now, and we are still without a MARM. Management positions are rarely given to the rank and file.

BACHELOR DEGREE IN MONKEY BUSINESS

Usually, a TM has to be at least a supervisor in some capacity before management will consider the person. Usually in dire straits will the company promote a nonsupervisor to a management position, unless favortism or cronyism is involved. The Personnel Manager position just received a lot of extra responsibility added to it according a job posting at #181 for it. Now, one needs a college degree, and has to have 1-2 years experience with payroll processing, and other things not required just a few months ago when the same position was available at a club farther north. So what have we learned? Favortism, cronyism, and emergencies will get you a management position. Merit, ambition, and dedication...not so much.

Greetings from #109 again!

OK, I stand corrected. We have a MARM. I wondered whose new name that was listed on the managers' mailbox. The funny thing is there are so many managers on the wall there is no room for his photo to show his background via the Ladder of Success. I counted 15 managers on the wall; he made number 16, and there was no space for him.

The recent RICM is very experienced, holding 8-9 different positions, including a senior position from which she stepped down.

BACHELOR DEGREE IN MONKEY BUSINESS

Greetings from #109 again!

I have no issue with the Superhero nomination idea. But wow! How much did BJ's invest in the production of those posters and such? The graphic art design is grandiose! The posters rival, and even outdo, some movie theater posters, I've seen. Meanwhile, clubs have forklifts that need repair, a shortage of forklift keys, broken pallet jacks, pb&j for lunch, hourly non management TM's get subpar raises, etc.

Not to knock TM's who give back to their communities, but what about the superheroes and superheroines who go without recognition, financial reward, and get taken advantage of because they are too good for their own good?

-The cashier who checks out more members than other cashiers
-The deli clerk who helps a line of members all alone
-The service desk TM who closes alone, and easily deals with member issues
-The liquor store TM left to fend for him/herself on major holidays
-The recovery clerk who doubles as a daytime ticketer
-The overnight ticketer who works more pallets than any other ticketer
-The food court clerk who helps a line of members all alone
-The TMs who do management work, only to have the credit stolen from them

There are many other examples, but you get the picture.

Maybe they would have better sales if they stopped cutting

BACHELOR DEGREE IN MONKEY BUSINESS

payroll, having enough night crew to stock the clubs, and more importantly enough cashiers.
Then maybe they can work on management teams that are not producing and start promoting from within instead of hiring off the street.

Well here we go again we are all working a million hours. Were allowed to come in early and stay late. Isn't that great ?! But when January comes they'll forget all about how many hours we worked and will think nothing of cutting all of our hours. Apparently we all need the money and we still need it in January. And whats up with these union meetings ? They shouldn't even have to worry about usw joining a union. Maybe they're worried because they know people are upset with how hard they work only to get yelled at for not doing someone elses job. Before when you were a cashier all you had to do was ring register. not any more ! Now you have to push carts in the rain. And the worst part is they don't even ask you they just tell you shut your light off and go push carts. And don't dare complain because then next week you will only get one day on your schedule. All we can hope for is CHANGE ! Good luck everybody and remember there are certain people there that do appreciate what you do. You will know who they are. Merry Christmas

Cor *and* ***Cur*** *BOTH started off as ticketers and worked their way up to their current positions. I would agree* ***Co*** *needs to grow up a little more,. however, he would be a better GM than the current ones running the show.*

Anonymous said that as long as the clubs " hit their numbers ", corporate will not care about day to day issues at the club

BACHELOR DEGREE IN MONKEY BUSINESS

level...

One anonymous person received a settlement check: *FYI, I got my settlement check today. South Florida.*

An anonymous post on the home office: *"They don't care about the employees, they just want to run a store with the bare minimum. The more they save the larger the bonus, so sure exploit the few good workers that you do have. If the store was properly staffed, and they stop giving the overtime to a select few then maybe they can manage the building."*

Anonymous thinks *"In order for BJ's to be a better company, they need to start with the home office."*

My club was opened in January and we're already running on bare bones staff. Our meat and deli depts have had almost a 100% turnover rate... and almost every other department is heading that way. Our customer service manager is the daughter of someone in corporate and went from being member services to CSM. The previous CSM was fired after she apparently threatened an FLS- let me tell you, this did NOT happen. She was told there was going to be a 24 hour investigation, and she was fired after 12 hours. The GM does NOTHING but sit in his office all day and has been on at least five week-long vacations since July. The assistant operations manager just pushes a cart with a clipboard and a soda doing "recovery".

I agree clermont fl location is exact same way the few good upper office people they had are gone now all that's left is

BACHELOR DEGREE IN MONKEY BUSINESS

incompetent idiots, it sounds a lot like straight across the boards Bjs managers need to go back to school!

Glassdoor.com website:
BJ's Wholesale Club Receiving Manager in Hudson, MA: (Current Employee)
Pros
The benefits offered are good, and the oppurtunity to receive free BJ's memberships for you and your family are a plus.

Cons
Compensation is generally very poor and treatment of employees seems to be poor as well. Managers are imcompetant and have a strong tendancy to mis-manage as well as micro-manage.

Advice to Senior Management
Gain a better understanding of the practices in each department as well as a respect for the amount of work that each employee puts in.

That had to have been written by the manager who makes the GM her breakfast every morning or the one who goes out and gets her lunch everyday. And yes, the GM does come down more then once. She comes down to get magazines to read in her office. I would go so far as to say almost everyone who works at 113 hates it. Morale is about as bad as it can get. Unless, like you say your one of the favorites. Your lucky if you get a hello out of these new managers. Doesn't anyone at corporate wonder why the turnover is so bad. Maybe when home office does a walk they shouldn't announce it so they can see what the store is really like.

BACHELOR DEGREE IN MONKEY BUSINESS

Jen Lyn she is the most UNPROFESSIONAL HR I have ever seen in my life. There was this manager was telling her what is going on in the club and about the GM. One second later after that manager walks out of the office, she walk straight to the GM and tell him everything about what that manager said about him. Isn't HR suppose to keep everything you says CONFIDENTIAL!!!!! . The upper level need to open their eyes and see she doesn't have ANY PROFESSIONALISM IN HER AT ALL and don't know how to do her jobs CORRECTLY. Jennifer lynch she really need to be FIRE!!!!!!

First of all **Jen Lyn** was hired by **Lor And,** so who's side do you really think she would be on. **Lor** has had her nieces hired at Bj's, and front door has been told not to write tnem up, by other managers. They come and go as they please and work what ever position they want within the store. **Lor** also sends her sister into the store to spy, which is very unprofessional. And the Alertline that is private is fake as hell. You type your problem up and you get a reply in 2-3 weeks contact your HR or Manager for details. How is that anonymous???? SHE IS **LOR'S** LACKEY!!!!!!

Will my manager see this hmm i wonder i work at club 165 why is the manager of the cash office mother to the girl who runs h.r. and mother to the girl who is the manager of membership

Cory started off as an overnight ticketer.
Rachel started off as a cashier. They came up through the ranks and paid their dues.
They are:
1. WORKING MANAGERS

BACHELOR DEGREE IN MONKEY BUSINESS

2. ACTUALLY CARE ABOUT PEOPLE
The rest of the Management at 13 ONLY care about themselves, and are doing as little as possible to keep their jobs in this difficult economy.
BJ's sucks ass. They open a new club and bring all the mid amangers but two from a troubled club along with the GM. I am one of the managers that is new to the company. And I can tell you this: from my short (and hopefully soon over) employment with BJ's they care nothing for the team members that make the club work. They are over paid hypocrites who think they are better than the team members. Got news for them all... if team members weren't running registers, standing at the door, sweeping the floors, checking in merchandise...etc... the club would not run. So take some of your fat bonuses and share it with the people who really run the club: THE TEAM MEMBERS.

I totally agree and find that it is so funny how a position is posted for anyone to bid for, but before they even post it they know who they are giving it to. That's ridiculous and not fair. Why waste someones time when you already know their bid is going right in the trash cause your friend does not have to put in a bid or do any work just talk about people and suck up to you and their in. I'm wondering what happened to the days when you had to work to earn your position? It's all been replaced by "the Buddy system". That's ridiculous!

I have noticed that whomever gets promoted at our club is a suck up to HR. Its just so many politics at our club. Our present HR sucked up to our last HR and took her job.I wish corporate would start just popping up at our club without telling our GM because all he do is lets the ones know who slacking that they are coming and when they get there, its like its supposed to be

BACHELOR DEGREE IN MONKEY BUSINESS

until they leave. They need to look at the people who got promoted and find out how they got promoted. Did they threaten to quit to get a promotion or did thier "BUDDY" put in a good word for them. Sometimes it sickens me and sometimes is just so funny.

Yes Bjs is a at work for will company. If you work their and you complain to any human resource idiot. Even if you are right and I gurrantee that you would be right. They will make up correctives to get ride off you like at club 39. Then when you write a letter to higher ups HR they will say that the decison is final although you never got to talk to any hire -up. Wake up people quit before you get fired. They always take the manager's word over any employee. Even when most managers are breaking the law. And do not even try to apply for a supervisor or maanger postion if you have experience. I had over 7 years of experience they will promise you that they will promote you. But then they will hire one of the friends of the supervisor and promote them. Then they will stick you on the register and trust me you will fail because they expect a perfect employee. Then you will get yelled at by the 20 year old supervisor, and they will be unprofessional and yell at you in front of the staff. Or you will have a 20 year manager trying to tell you what to do. Do not ever work thier unless you want to collect an unemployment check

I used to enjoy going to work at club 167. Since the management change to GM **Way Sim**, now I dread having to go to work. We are constantly micro managed under Waynes World. Nights are rough enough to deal with getting an entire Club ready for the next day, just to be treated like kindergarten children. Most night there are only 3 ticketers instead of a full night crew. At this point, we are kept from doing our jobs to its

BACHELOR DEGREE IN MONKEY BUSINESS

entirety due to BS. Management now lock up the clothing cage so that simple items like hangers are unaccessable to overnight crew. The symbals that are needed to do the signage, check stock and code changes are also locked away. How can you expect to us to do our jobs when you remove the tools that are needed? I have had the unfortunate priviledge of personally being screamed at by **Way** on muliple occasions, of which I had no control over the issues. If your not a favorite or "pet" that has coffee or hot chocolate brought in for you by management then you already know your time there will be minimal.

As far as making a complaint, **Jen Lyn** with HR is and always will be for the GM, so it is pointless, unless you file a Formal grievance.

Mtt M. one of the overnight specialists, sits on his forklift most of the night and delegates some of his duties to ticketers so that he has time to chat, then every morning takes credit for the work. Pallet counts don't mean anything because he erases and reduces counts of ticketers and adds them to his own. Waynes World will be the downfall of Club 167.

I have worked for BJ's for over a decade. Yes, I know I am crazy for staying with a company like this one for so long. (I have my reasons.) Any how this guy **Mtt** who thinks he runs shit decides to take upon himself to do other peoples' work including mine. He acts like he is a saint and is always doing what the boss tells him. No reality he does basically nothing until 6 am. That is when he acts like he is pulling his weight. Duping all managers into thinking his work ethic is like this all night, which isn't the case by any means. On top of that he will open the back door to let me in and as soon as I step foot in the

BACHELOR DEGREE IN MONKEY BUSINESS

club, he is arguing with me stirring the pot. **Mtt** thinks he is on top of the world. He is always right about all topics in his mind. It is disgusting and I'm quite frankly sick and tire of his nonsense.

I worked at Club 167, we have a Verizon kiosk in the store and the representative of Verizon was locked in the store until after store hours. All managers were gone and the store's alert was set of. Of course the alert went off and the alert company never called to see what the issue was. A night crew member arrived and saw this Verizon rep still in the store. How does this happen? A lazy manager who clearly doesn't know how to make sure to check the club before leaving. Embarrassing if you ask me.

Why am I posting anonymously? Because I'm most likely already on their list of "trouble makers" who asks too many intelligent questions along with telling other employees to question what they are told without checking policies.

NEVER complain to Human Resources about a manager because they go right back to the manager. I guarantee you NOTHING will be done and that manager will make your life HELL till you quit or they fire you on a trumped up charge. And I'm not talking about lazy employees looking for a free ride. LMAO!

I was at 13 recently, and of the 4 managers on duty, only 2 were actually working (**Cor** & **Rac**). The 2 that were not working were driving the FLS' crazy. There is NO reason why these 2 non working managers (**Vic** & **Cyn**) could not have helped out

Chapter Five: Masters Degree in Monkey Business

This particular night, near the end of November, the Overnight Food Specialist told me endcaps were back to being six feet high. Just a few months ago, corporate told us to make them four feet high because all of the skyscraper stacking was taking time away from other duties ticketers/stock clerks could be doing, and from the management responsibilities the specialists could be doing.

Was the change back to the original height for sales reasons, or cosmetic? No answer. As long as the item is there, and it is in demand, no matter how tall or how short you stack it, if they want it, they will buy it. But if the item is a miss instead of a hit, you could stack it to look as beautiful as topiary or origami and nobody would touch it. When will the geniuses in the White House understand such simple concepts?

There are people with advanced degrees, making six figures and making the most absurd decisions. Sounds a lot like our government. In 1995, 1996, and 2013, Congress caused the government to shut down. Hundreds of national parks and many governmental agencies closed, and hundreds of

MASTERS DEGREE IN MONKEY BUSINESS

thousands of government employees went unpaid.[2] All because of a failure to make good decisions.

A few months ago this year [2016], senior management decided to use a new method to save on payroll. It decided to give hourly team members forced vacations! It also instituted forced of sick time. One overnight ticketer checked his weekly schedule, and saw he had no days or hours. He asked management about it, and was told he was on vacation next week. He didn't fill out a Time Off Request Form, so how was that possible? Some people would be glad, but most wouldn't. The guy hadn't planned for a vacation, so he hadn't saved up for one. He spent his week off, working his second job during the day, and staying home at night with nothing to do. Five days and 37.5 hours of vacation gone from his vacation time without his consent. One of my friends who is a meat cutter, was already on vacation and out of town. His meat manager left him a message to take another week off. Overnight Specialists were asked to take a vacation day or sick day off, to save on payroll. Managers were asked to take extra time off too. Vacation and sick time are paid from balances that are not charged to the club. People were upset, but didn't report it to their local Human Resources Business Partner (HRBP), or Home Office.

And why would they? The call to do that, came from approval much higher than club level.

Some other creative cost cuts came in the form of demoting an MSS because she could not be flexible with her schedule. She had started a second job, which meant she could not be as available to BJs as she was before that. She was already part time with no benefits, and had children. Add insult to injury,

MASTERS DEGREE IN MONKEY BUSINESS

management demoted her back to cashier after she filled out an availability form based upon her hours at her other job. This came under the new regime. Before a new GM came with his crew, that was never an issue. But that was not the worse situation. An MSS who transferred there in 2011 after her location closed had a schedule that allowed her to care for her daughters, one of which was diagnosed with cancer.

Previous management knew about her situation, and took it into consideration when it came ot her schedule. There were more than enough people with her title who could fill in where she could not. But then new management arrived, and mandated that all full-time team members had to be flexible in terms of their schedules. They didn't demote her, but reduced her hours to 30 before lunches were taken. That left her with 27.5 hours, and that meant she no longer qualified for benefits. Employees at BJs must work at least 30 hours to be entitled to benefits. She had a previous incident with an newly transferred OPS. She was from up north, and had a unique accent. So when she says certain names, it can sometimes sound odd. One particular day, she paged the OPS. He took exception to how she pronounced his name and made it a point to confront her about it. He went as far as to enunciate it to her! This particular OPS was your stereotypical, macho juice monkey. One who worked out, dressed like he was in GQ magazine, and would not hesistate to beat his chest to anyone he outranked. He was Italian, and extremely proud of it. His tirade left her in tears. But he got his the last day he was scheduled to work before another transfer. The GM had him inventory the entire freezer. It was at least a 12 hour day and night for him. He also had plans to have brunch with his mother. By the end of the count, he was beyond exhausted.

MASTERS DEGREE IN MONKEY BUSINESS

So as you see, this MSS went through more than any employee should have to endure just to keep a job. Sadly, she took as much as she could. Because her schedule was so much of a hassle for management, she made one last schedule change, and scheduled herself to resign January 1st.

The irony of BJs schedules is those who have paid their dues and put in work over the years, receive less consideration for the need of schedules that accomodate their life situations than new hires. New hires whose applications do not require weekends off, or day shifts only, end up getting exactly that. The same meat cutter who told me his meat manager was going to write him up for following his own direction, told me how all the young guys in his department get more weekend days off, or more opening shifts than he did. He had to request weekend days, or opening shifts with his current meat manager, and ones prior to him. I understood him. My only consolation was to tell him he was too good to have weekend days off, and too good to not close so often. He laughed and agreed, but still said it wasn't fair.

Here is something for those high up in the BJs food chain. Stop doing was doesn't work, and do more of what does work. I listened to a story that author, businessman, and motivational speaker, Bob Proctor, mentioned that very thing in his "The Science of Getting Rich" seminar.

A man had an engineering business doing about $10 million annually. His widow wanted nothing to do with the business, and never visited it. After his death, things slowed down. People thought she would sell the business, but instead she did

MASTERS DEGREE IN MONKEY BUSINESS

something else. One day, she went into the company, and met with all the department heads. She asked them three simple questions:

What are you doing?
What works?
What doesn't?

After talking with all of them, she told them one thing. Stop doing what doesn't work, and spend the time on what does work. That simple directive took the company from $10 million in sales to $25 million.

Bob stated that just that advice alone could be worth millions to the people at his seminar. Maybe former CEO Laura Sen, and now, CEO, Chris Baldwin, should attend a Bob Proctor, Brian Tracy, or Tony Robbins seminar. Or watch and listen to old Jim Rohn and Zig Ziglar seminar video and audio.

Question...

Why does corporate ask for cost saving suggestions, only to ignore them even though numbers for saving money were quoted chain wide to a regional manager?
My aunt works at BJ's and suggested something to do with un-necessary code signs(?) that have to be changed.

Why do you ignore cost saving suggestions and yet keep bragging about all the money you are making?

Couldn't you be hiring extra help with these savings in paper cost? Just a suggestion if you are looking to make some

MASTERS DEGREE IN MONKEY BUSINESS

changes to save money.
P.S... I'm saying something because my aunt is afraid of ramifications from management if they posted it. Sad, itn't it?

Why dont they try working on the existing stores they have new instead if diverting resources to a prototype that may or may not work. This is not the economy to be testing new ideas like that. Many of the existing clubs need to be udpdated. If they have the money to do all of this, why not kick some of that back down to the team members who are keeping this ship afloat instead of cutting hours.

Have you ever done a remodel? I have and the way corporate does things, it is amazing the remodels ever get done.

I remember re-doing the ethnic foods area 7 times and when it was said and done, time number 3 looked identical to time number 7.

We also completed the project 3 weeks ahead of schedule AND under budget. We did not even get a thank you. MANY others ran over time and budget. Corporate did not seen to care.

Nice responses from the Home office about hours. Its obvious you don't work at club level if you think the payroll is sufficient. Some clubs do get the payroll they need, most do not. Thats a simple fact. If you do not have the hours available for replenishment, cashiers, etc, you will not have sales.

Payroll is the number one expense HO can control, but running clubs on skeleton crews is no way to positivly increase the

MASTERS DEGREE IN MONKEY BUSINESS

bottom line.

This company has to decide what it wants to be. Dose it want to be a warehouse club, a grocery store or a dept store. It sufferes from a Identity crisis, as seen by the many new programs that get implimented and then pushed to the side when a new idea hits them. So far, they have failed to really stick with any program long enough to actually see them through to the end.

I agree... what the hell are you thinking opening a new club in this recession? I'm well aware that it's all about the money. You need to look at what you are doing to the clubs that are doing well in spite of this recession.

This penalizing a region with cutbacks and layoffs because several of the clubs (in the region) are not doing well is ludicrous! I thought when they shuffled and/or fired CEO's at corporate level that the dead wood was gone and things would get better! But silly me assumed there were intelligent people running this company. It seems the "instant gratification" mentality survived at head quarters! When are you going to realize you are distroying your own futures? Haven't you learned anything with the ecomony going down the toilet? Opening a new club will NOT fix the problems with this chain. Looking at individual clubs, maintaining the ones that are making the money makes sense! We are 'carrying' the low volume clubs like Mays Landing, Voorhees, etc. This makes no sense what-so-ever!

I don't know why I even bother venting here, because the ones running this site (home office, for those who haven't figured it out yet!) are just checking to see how far they can go before

MASTERS DEGREE IN MONKEY BUSINESS

they throw us a bone to shut us up for a few months before making another idiotic move to make money at our expense!

I worked for BJ's in the Natick, MA Home Office and glad I have finally decided to leave. Senior Management needs to pull their heads out of their butts.. Who decides to place non industry experience personnel in SVP Management Roles....Loss Prevention now has Logistics, Logistics has I.T., Flnance has Merchandising... Best thing they could do, is get rid of the old timers, and kiss ass Management and get fresh blood... Hey BJ's, grab your knees, bend over and kiss your Company good-bye...

Chapter Six: Flinging Poo at You

Overnight Specialists written up while on their vacation for something their peers did. That sounds almost like the hit movie, "Friday", when Craig got fired on his day off! Mass layoffs in a failed effort to trim the fat. As much as clubs cut hours, they still cry about being over on them. Huh? Well, let me paraphrase an old adage. When you clench your hand tight to hold onto the money you have, your hand will not be open to receive any new money you may get. Management position consolidations which lead to more stress and more attrition. Lots of misplaced blame. Person C does something wrong. The boss confronts person E about it, and person E has nothing to do with it. When you point your finger, the other four point back at you. BJ's is full of misplaced blame. It is a proven method of absolving one's self from guilt.

Whenever a "big wig" is supposed to visit. Every day manager scrambles like the place is on fire! But why? If they did their jobs 90 percent of the time, then it would only take 10 percent to make up for it when the big bosses come. So what do the day managers do? They force cashiers to stay late, cleaning every nook and cranny around the cash registers, doing go backs/reshops 100 percent, they hire independent contractor to strip, clean, and wax the floors, and sometimes purchase new

FLINGING POO AT YOU

furnishing. This costs lots of budget money. After all of that hooplah, guess what happens. Nothing. Nobody shows, or if they do, they bypass the location that wanted to pass the white glove inspection. Senior management then drastically cuts hours to make up for all the overage in payroll and overspending they did for the contractors.

Bakery, meat, and deli departments make sure they have full staffs all hours of the day. So if the big boss comes, it will appear as though they always run the store with that capacity, the same for cashiers. They will call people on their days off, and ask them to come in, or see if they want overtime. Those who need the money do it, also those who are new and don't know they can decline. Others, who value their time more than the money, stay put.

The receiving dock suddenly looks immaculate, which is a feat. But after the dog and pony show, it goes right back to looking like garbage.

Overnight becomes a future ground zero. Many specialists ride around on their mechanical horses/chariots, and drop the house on the ticketers. Stuff comes out of the steel you didn't even know BJ's sold: car bumpers, big marble tile, astro turf, traffic lights, ditch diggers. Ok, I exaggerated, but some do some go overboard. If a pallet is missing three cases, some drop a single layer just to make the pallet full again. That is a fact! Night crew is fully staffed for a good "pack out", and overtime is available again. Pallets have to be laser pointer straight, signs cannot be crooked or missing, and the sales floor has to look like grand opening. They tell you to stay as long as you want until everything looks perfect. The following week, it's chop, chop, chop on the hours. Leave on time. Hell, leave early if you can!

When there is nobody of importance coming, the paradox is the specialists drop more pallets when short staffed, and less pallets when fully staffed. It is almost as if they want to kill the ticketers. But only the good ones. They coddle the ones who can't cut the mustard. Overnight specialists actually get pissed when "beast" and "monster" overnight ticketers are off, or call out, and they have to drop pallets on the slower ones and the "monkey boys". When the beasts and monsters come back to work, their areas don't look packed out. Why? Because the overnight specialists had the slackers just recover their sections, or they only dropped a few pallets for them. Now that the good ones are back, the overnight specialists drop the house!

We are all supposed to be interchangeable, meaning able to work other sections that are not our designated ones, if needed. So if a "beast" or "monster" gets 50-70 pallets dropped on him, so should anyone else who works his area in his absence. Not in the alternate reality at BJs.

News comes down for high above, and is delivered on stone tablets. Senior Merchants leave mega crap loads of notes [think of them as overnight homework assignments] for the overnight specialists, especially the Overnight Non-Food Specialist. The company is obsessed with resets at the club level. Resets are the things that drive you crazy as a member/customer, and get employees that much closer to a rubber room, especially those who have to do them. You see them in all retail environments, some more than others. One

FLINGING POO AT YOU

day, gardening supplies are in aisle four. The next day, they are in aisle five. Two weeks later, they are gone! Where did they go? Most likely, up in the steel or reserve [the area above the sales floor where you see merchandise on wrapped pallets]. Resets are annoying, but are not bad...when you have the available staff for them. Or when you have more time to focus on them, and not a myriad of other things.

Senior Merchants are notorious for wanting resets done when there is hardly any staff, 1-2 trucks full of merchandise to receive, and only one overnight specialist. They don't ask the GM to stop the truck so the team can do a basic minimum of drops, and then focus solely on the reset. Once that is done, they can get the sales floor cleared of pallets, and ready for business that day. No. That would be too easy, not to mention, considerate.

Recently, a Senior Merchant came in all juiced up on his Monster Energy drinks he religiously brings to work, and started a major reset around 6:15 AM with three ticketers. All but one was scheduled to leave at 7 AM. One by one, the ticketers quietly made their way out of the aisle, and to the time clock. The one left, who came in at 5 AM, ended up doing the reset with the Senior Merchant until 12 PM that day. Failing to plan, is planning to fail.

Another bad practice is how the daytime managers and daytime hourly employees eat compared to the night crew. Daytime managers use club money to buy themselves lunch, and then eat it in the HR Manager's office, which oversees the entire floor. They eat like Gods on Mount Olympus. If there are any leftovers, they put them out to pasture in the break room. If

FLINGING POO AT YOU

there is something special going on one month, such as Cinco De Mayo, Fourth of July, etc., the club uses money to buy enough food for the opening and closing shift employees. By the time the night crew arrives, the leftovers look like animal carcasses! Large and small flies land on the uncovered trays and open platters. There is so much personally bought/brought employee food in the fridge, there is no room to put the leftovers for safe keeping. The fridge food looks more like garbage that someone should throw away, but didn't. Some clubs look out for their night crews, and put the leftover food in the HR office for them. Other clubs give the night crew club money to spend for food whether it be from the club or ordered from places such as Miami Subs Grill or Papa John's.

Alright, let's hit the blog to see how the deck is stacked against employees at BJs.

To the idiots that think it is all about sales - You guys must pay absolutely no attention to the company that you work for! Yes, sales are extremly important but without our members we will not have any sales! Payroll is based off a combination of MFI (membership fee income) and sales. So I suggest we make our clubs a more pleasurable easy place for our members to shop, and we might see our payroll increase. This means FLS's don't hang around at the podium getting mad when self checkouts flash or a cashier needs you, its not the cashier but the member that needs your assistance, I am quite sure that the cashier would not call you if they didn't have to, seeing how some of you guys act! If an MOD is paged to Member services dont call the desk team back and ask "what they want", again it is not the team member that needs you but the member! The new program OTO (own the outcome) that came down from HO is a

FLINGING POO AT YOU

GREAT idea, we are in business for the Members not ourselves and until you guys realize that without our members your paycheck is not possible you will not see an increase in any of our clubs payroll! So stop the whining about not having any hours and just do what you were hired to do!

You are acting like 40 pallets is a lot in a shift. On 1 shift in Mays Landing, I cleared 70 pallets without assistance. Not boasting or bragging, but you do what it takes to get the job done, especially when the Regional VP pulls you out of your club to go down there and WANTS IT DONE ASAP....

LP is one of the hardest manager positions. We are stuck between a rock and a brick wall. The RLP tells you one thing which is policy and the seniors tell you to do it a different way, or tell your people what to do. So what can you do? Tell the regional? Then thee seniors get mad at you and you look like a tattle tail. ITS AWFUL. I REGRET THIS MOVE 100%

I've been a LP manager and it's not that tough. Suggestion - train one of your front or back door TM's to do daily counts. They do not take that long. They don't have to be 100% everyday which frees you up to concentrate on auditable counts (High Shrink and Jewelry). Athough many people don't like Michele, she will back you up! If she tells you to do something and your GM or Srs won't comply, let her know. If anyone gets mad at you or calls you a tattle tale, screw them. You are there to do a job, not make friends! I have never been a RICM, but that seems like the hardest managers positon. They are in charge of 3 departments. All depts have detailed paperwork work which is all on the Operational Audit plus they have to do department counts, jewelry returns, 950 transfers

FLINGING POO AT YOU

etc...

The problem with bus is not the workers. It's the upper management. The business has changed but the concept of how to get the job done has not. They use the term "PACK OUT" like Rome can be built in a day all while they are cutting hours. There's just a disconnect between upper management and what it actually takes to get the job done. Workers are too often used as pawns for managers to make themselves look good. This one manager named "Sicone" is just the worst. I've personally haven't had any negative dealings with him but watching him start trouble everywhere he goes makes you wonder what does bus consider a good manager. The concept that if the workers are complaining then the manager is doing his or her job is just insane. But we have what we have.

What happened to all of you? While Sen negotiated her and others golden parachutes we sit and wait, doing nothing to protect our interests? So as they say in management "you need to get more out of your people". They don't care if you go home exhausted and broke, they don't balance work loads and staff, they just simply want more out of you. Try being a ticketer working water aisles 3 or more night in a row while the favorites go to cereal or electronics. Or try being a ticketer in food, hand stacking everynight, it's like being a brick layer building the great wall of China. There's no balance, it's all "get more out of the ticketers".

I see a lot of comments with no names. Why bother. I work for club 139 and his hell. We barely able to use do bathroom on nightshift. We not even allowed to go to the vending machines for a snack or a cold drank. We are told it takes to much time to

FLINGING POO AT YOU

get a snack or drank. If n e out there want inside info on the treatment of club 139.. Man up woman up and leave a name. Alphonso savoris

Ha Ha Ha been gone from bj's for a while and i see things just don't change...i feel bad for the workers esp. the overnight crews that have to work like slaves and still get more work dumped on them..If they just treated people with some respect and not like garbage they find they would have better running stores ..Treat someone like crap their going to work like crap but that's what they want

- Inconsistent hours (30-33 hours per week for fifth consecutive month; with the odd extra hour here and there; and it's back to thirty two weeks before Memorial Day - WTF?)
^^ And that's on a 'full-time' basis.
- Hourly pay sucks (over $11+ WITH the shift differential. And I've been at my club for nearly four years now.)
- Quite the skeletal night crew here at club #096. With only a handful of people (3 present to cover all three zones on a GOOD night). On bad nights (which have been much too common lately), there's only 2, or even 1 person to cover the whole store. Only in such dire straits do the managers recover a zone. And sometimes, there's only one manager present to do freezer/misc. trucks, boom everything off the latter, plus fill THREE zones (mainly holes).
- Too many corners cut and not enough people/hours. Store looks like absolute crap because the CONSTANT half-assed recovery. NO incentive to move faster than you are capable of moving (6/6.5 hour shifts). Expectations to do MORE for LESS, and I won't do that.
- And if you're not a faster recovery person - you're apparently

FLINGING POO AT YOU

useless. Try and do your job the right way (albeit it taking longer), yet you get reprimanded. Fill what you're supposed to NOT fill with the forklift, and you get reprimanded. I notice things that should be filled, yet they don't. And if THEY did not bring them down to be filled, then you get reprimanded. To hell with that bull.
- Team 'Politics' and 'Intricacies'. Sick of that.
- Forcing someone to work a department they dislike working in because they don't 'feel' like hiring a replacement. That crap just causes a sharp DROP in morale and motivation from Team Member.

I worked at BJ's Wholesale Club/Company for a decade. I see all this comments that pertain to unfair treatment and unequal opportunity. I will not state what Club number and location I worked at, but it is still all the same. It is very simple to comprehend. People that are willing to have no backbone, never argue about a single thing, always say yes and be worked like a rented mule, you will most likely always have a place at BJ's, no matter how hard you work or don't work. Favorites are preferred at BJ's. Don't even try reading the handbook because many of the managers and most importantly the GMs that take the place of others have their own policies to follow. Some don't have anything to do with what the handbook states. Taking your problems to Regional HR Managers don't help out your cause either. They stand up for every manager. It is one big family and we are the ones that get chewed out for doing the grunt/dirty work. Seniority doesn't make a difference why it applies to moving up with the company and applying for more responsible/important positions.

FLINGING POO AT YOU

You know what cracks me up? Every club is forging signature to pass an audit. Ray wasent hitting golf clubs all day. Stop making excuses, things will never change that way. Stick to the real facts. Talk to the deli guy who has 10 people in line and is working alone. Doesnt get his break. Talk to the reciever, who has to unblock the carbord dumpster before he even starts to unload his trucks. Talk to fls, who never has a lunch because a manager is too lazy to stand on the frontline for a half hour. How about the meatcutter who has to cut meat, wrap it, pack it out, pull chicken out of the oven, package it, put a truck away, pack deli wall, and island cases. How about the produce guy who cant get his truck off the receiving dock because their is so much crap on it. What about the overnite crew, who works no less than a ten hour day. These are the people who should be bitching on this. These are the people, who make a club run. Not the managers, looking at lunch menue's at 10:00am.

My wife worked for this Shit company for 17 years. Now she is being forced out. Everyone with time better watch your backs. There will be lawsuits. I know of 5 people that will be suing. I see A class-action in their future!
they made a list
of bullshit. they have been firing people with 4 weeks vacation. Her store allow has fired 5 people so far. There is a meat cutter with 22 years that will be going next. They made him order fish for lent and he told them it wouldn't sell. then when it didn't he got written up.

yeah the longer your there the more they want to get rid of you...i was there over 15 years did everything they asked me and more ..all of a sudden started mickey mousing me on raises and write ups..almost 15 years without a write up all of a

FLINGING POO AT YOU

sudden boom you were 5 mins late (who cares when its 10pm at night) writeup.but they forget the hours i stayed to bail them out when they were in trouble

STOP THE WHINING !!!!!!!
Who ever said life was fair!!!!!

How about all the Overnight Managers who worked prior to the cutoff date? They get nothing !!!!!

I had a SENIOR Merchandise Manager who would make lists 6 pages long, and expect it ALL to get done that night. It got to the point the GM got involved and told the Senior " Lets see you get the 6 page list done along with everything else to be completed, and you will do it TONIGHT!!! He came in, did not complete his own list and guess what....Never had a 6 page list again

Be glad for any amount you receive.

Club 028 again.

[quote]Has anyone seen any type of overnight Specialist's tasks list with dead lines?[/quote]

I remember seeing overnight manager lists. Man, the GM or the Merch would lay it on thick for them. And with our club being so small, and no real time for forklift training, the overnight managers had to do the drops, truck, their lists, and boom up. And if there was only one manager on duty because the other was off, he really caught heck. Their 10-6 was more like 10-9, 10-10, 10-11.

FLINGING POO AT YOU

Now that they are Overnight Specialists and on the clock, their lists are much smaller. It also helps that the club is making Lead positions available and hiring forklift drivers. There is still no real time for forklift training. But those who know the forklift step up and teach others who show willingness to learn it.

Regarding the settlement, its just that--a settlement. BJ's legal team will do their own computations vs. Klafter Olsen & Lesser LLP's computations. Klafter Olsen & Lesser LLP may have wanted $16 million. BJ's legal team may have countered and said, we are prepared to offer $11 million with no litigation.

Chapter Seven: Monkey Wrench

As a manager, specialist, or hourly team member, you strive to do your best. Frequently, your best is met with obstacles, which is par for the course at any company. But when the company itself creates those obstacles, it makes you question the company. And it makes you question yourself. If you work for idiots, what does that make you? I think Obi-Wan Kenobi said it best in Star Wars, "Whose more foolish, the fool, or the fool who follows him"?

When there were a countless number of pictures gracing the the wall of each BJ's [BJ's Ladder of Success], as if they were heads on Mount Rushmore, each night, two managers closed unless one called out. It only took one daytime manager to open a store, and then others came later. On Mondays, when they had their Monday morning meeting, all managers were on duty.
But after January 2016, when the big purge took place from Home Office to club level, stores went from two manager closings, to one manager closings. They eliminated four mid managers positions, renamed and consolidated them to perform dual roles. Receiving and Inventory Control Manager [RICM], Asset Protection Manager [APM] formerly known as Loss Prevention Manager [LPM], Customer Service Manager

MONKEY WRENCH

[CSM], and Membership Acquisitions and Retention Manager [MARM] positions became Asset Control Manager [ACM], and Member Service Manager [MSM]. Personnel Manager [PM] was renamed Human Resource Manager [HRM]. BJ's renamed the Front Line Supervisor [FLS] position to Member Service Supervisor [MSS], and gave them some management responsibilities, one of which, was to close with the only manager left in the building. Every so often, two managers would close, but usually only if needed.

That is a far cry from what BJ's does to its overnight specialists. They often schedule them to work 6-9 days straight without a day off in between. And that is a normal schedule! That is with a second overnight, or even third overnight specialist on the roster, and none of them on vacation. Some clubs have only two overnight specialists, so when one goes on vacation, the other has to run things all alone. If the Gods on Mount Olympus feel gracious, they may pull an overnight specialist from another club to assist the one working alone. Sometimes, the Assistant Manager Merchandise/Senior Merchant will cover the remaining overnight specialist's off days. A good Senior Merchant will volunteer for that. Not so good ones must be told to do it.

Daytime mangers never see a week with them working so many days straight. The only way overnight specialists can avoid that is to talk to the Senior Merchant about it, or the GM. By the way, they do hourly employees the same way. Ever since BJ's went to an automatic schedule, consideration went right out the window. One press of a button saves 40 hours of manually making a schedule. Sometimes it over schdules employees, sometimes it under schedules employees, and

MONKEY WRENCH

sometimes it doesn't schedule them at all.

While on the subject of schedules. Managers and supervisors are in charge of scheduling team members accordingly. Many times, they sabotage each other, and won't breathe a word about it to whoever is affected. It is usually OPS Managers and Human Resource Managers who do this because they are in charge of the budget and payroll. They will shift hours from one department to another, and won't tell the managers or supervisors who lost hours from their payroll for their department. And just like children, they will act clueless when asked about it. This cluelessness is also something some Senior Merchants do when their overnight specialists ask them how did they get scheduled so many days back-to-back without a day off, or when they have to run the show alone on busy nights, or when they have only one ticketer, or none. BJ's has a universal culture. So nearly every response is "That's not the schedule I made. Someone must've changed it." One huge fault in the BJ's culture is lack of communication. It was the case when there were many faces on the BJ's Ladder of Success. And it is still the case with fewer faces.

Let us take a look at what bloggers had to say about being hit with a BJ's monkey wrench.

As a FORMER BJ'S Manager, I realized that I would never get to be a GM because I did not play the game. Some of the BEST managers are NO LONGER
employed with BJ'S, for a variety of reasons, and what you have today that call themselves managers would not last outside of BJ'S WORLD..

MONKEY WRENCH

As a current manager, I just want you to know that some of us do try, and do care... we are not all villians, and heartless. I have worked for those kind of people with this company also, and I try every day not to be like that... it is a fight, when we get pushed against when we try to do the right thing for our people. The greatest gift they can give me is for those that work for me to tell me they are glad to see me every day, and that somehow me being there helps them somehow. If only all of us thought like that it would be a far better place... hopefully someday, until then, I do my best to take care of my peeps! ;) and as long as they care, thats all the accalade I need.

Oh, and I have worked outside BJ's, and survived quite well, but I happen to love some of the people I work with, they make my day better, so I try to do the same.

I do agree however that over the years we have lost some extremely good people, but also some bad eggs... so I guess you have to take both to even out, and hope we end up better in the end.

take care everyone, I will continue to be positive.

I worked for Bj's as a cashier for about a month. I told them this was a part time job for me because I already had a full time job and I only wanted 3 nights a week. What did they do? Schedule me for 5 or 6 nights a week. I worked in retail before and it's still the same. During my interview the personnel manager bragged about how much their sales were up during the recession then on the other hand said they could only afford to pay me $7.65 an hour. Then I had a second interview with the general manager and he, knowing that my full time job was/is a union job bashed unions saying everyone here does everything and there's no such thing as seniority or union wages. Regardless of all that I was offered the cashier job and I accepted it,

MONKEY WRENCH

because I figured I could use the extra money for Christmas. I had to quit because of too many hours and I felt they treat their employees like teenagers. I mean you cannot even accept a check without approval for your FLS. Even when the FLS tells you to take the check, thet doesn't mean it won't bounce. The cash registers are in dissary missing buttons and the scanner doesn't work, I had to scan everything with the scan gun which makes it harder for a new cashier. I thought while I was on the register missing just about all the buttons, doesn't this place have a contract with IBM to maintain these registers? When I asked that very same question, I was told just to deal with it. I didn't deal with it, I quit because I felt I was treated like a teenager. But oh well, that's just the way it went. If the adult workers were smart they organize for union representation. That way they would get a lot more respect from management.

To the pee-on that loves working at BJ's club. Try working night stocking and see if you still love this place. BJ's manual says you are not allowed to lift over 30 lbs without help and if you do so and get injured you will not covered by BWC. their so called 30 lb rule is a joke. I had to lift from 50-70lbs all night long continueously on my 8 hr shift lifting and stocking the shelves,ask for help you are shown the door, training says they provide a back support brace too, NOT!!!!! They do not go by any of their own guidelines and could care less about their employees. If you're not going to stick to your own rules then why have them in print and why make us sit through 4 hours of training because it doesn't mean crap. You were either a door person or cashier if you love this stupid place and no doubt never did any of the real work while you were there.Work overnight stock and see how in love you still are with this place.

MONKEY WRENCH

I work in a club that I'm forced to cut demo shifts, close out demos that are never performed all because Im not given enough payroll to complete!
Some days I have one person doing multiple demos!
I speak to others at other clubs and it's the same everywhere! The companies paying for these demos to be performed need to know they are getting ripped off!
Alot of the demo product is used to feed managers on a regular basis or to be used for events.. Not what it's intended for!
BJ's should be ashamed of themeselves for asking us to do such things!

As of July 28th, 2014; nothing has changed.

I am currently a zone lead in the club. I watch as the zone 2 manager, zone 2 lead (who apparently is also the "liquor lead" which is a joke at 055) and both when they're both on on the same day get shit on repeatedly as they "don't help other zones succeed". It's a joke. They both help other zones; do THEIR RESETS for them, while the zone 2 manager is doing their reset, the supposed "liquor lead" is zoning and filling seasonal, chips, nuts and dropping for the liquor vendors AND filling beer, the "liquor lead" is driving for other zones and being called repeatedly during the day because "they weren't there to drop for vendors, it looks terrible for the regional and the senior merchant and/or receiver dropped product for them" when they come in at 2am and leave at 10am (the vendors come around 6am as I'm leaving) and they drop for the person in clothing and books, because no one else can drop for them as they "don't have time", but they get bi---ed at.
I don't get it. One night, between seasonal, nuts, chips and beer, they called 53 pallets (over 3 stacks stacks of 18 blue or

MONKEY WRENCH

red pallets) and all the opening senior managers could say was "can you kill any more pallets? You need to work faster" (if you ever worked seasonal, you should know how impossible it is to put out more than one box of this, one box of that) Besides him and the zone manager, there's no one else in that zone. They seem to think that one of the people they hired 2 months ago works that zone, but was taken by the zone 3 manager almost immediately because "they needed more people". They have 3 other forklift drivers and 3 other ticketers. Zone 1 has 2 drivers, the manager, and 3 ticketers. Zone two has the zone 2 lead/liquor lead and the zone manager. I'm not including the clothing and book people, since they're THE SAME PERSON.

I've recently looked into going back to my old club; 119. The senior merchant and gm were kind and treated their employees fair. Hell, they came in ON THEIR DAYS OFF the day before Thanksgiving and Christmas so we could get out early enough to sleep and spend time with our families. The clowns at 055? Forget it. Good luck getting any time off if you work over night.

I recently told them about a friend I may be having surgery for. They told me "I couldn't have it done" because "I was needed". Guess what; I'm needed by them too. You treat me with respect, I treat you with respect. I follow that rule to a T; you treat me like crap, you get treated like crap and get crap work in return. Beg and plead me to stay all you want now; you'll get nothing from now on.

BJ's in Mass is RETARDED; When they are putting payroll budgets together they are giving more payroll to clubs based on which VP lives in their town, this is an absurd level of thinking all it does is paint a false picture in the real BJ's world in other

MONKEY WRENCH

clubs. What company TAKES payroll away during the timeframe between Thanksgiving and Christmas?? Apparently BJ's is that company, agree with poster stating Cornell is trying to micromanage the stores..try working in an area where Cornell can pop in at any moment any day any time, I don't think I have ever met anybody that lives in more of a pretend world than him. The major problem with BJ's right now resides at the ZONE VP level, as long as we have ZONE VPs that have no balls to stick up for the retail side of the business to Cornell this company won't run at its full potential. Almost a box a day of email communication, we are being over communicated to it is near impossible to even have the time to read all of the memos. Somebody throw us a life line...

Beware!!!
Bj's is showing a profit at the expense of cutting payroll and expecting under paid managers to pick up the slack! How is a manager supposed to manage when they are forced to work behind membership counter or act as a front line supervisor ect... Wake up!!!! can anyone
honestly say they have gotten good service at a bjs?
All they care about is is MFI=Membership fee income!
Controlling payroll at any expense!
and being Audit ready!
And if you look at the audit it has very little to ensure its members are taken care of!

As soon as you defend yourself because of being mistreated or you can't do your job 100% because they pull people out of your department to help other departments,you are labeled the enemy and all of a sudden a bad employee.Who the hell wants to work for a company that treats their workers like shit unles

MONKEY WRENCH

you are an ass kisser and keep your mouth shut?

one of the worst jobs i had i was a meat wrapper and one day they need help in the deli so they decided the meat dept had to help. I made the mistake of doing a good job and ended up working in the awful deli a couple days a week. I was also put in charge of the rotisararie so im doing 3 peoples jobs and getting paid the same as when i started. I had prior deli exp and ended being the main deli employee the auditor came and showed me somthing that was not acceptable and i said so what this isn't my fucking dept i don't care, especiall since some of the people in the deli are getting paid 12 dollars an hour cause they got hired when the store opened so im pissed. I ask the manager who is a giant douche bag for a raise since i am doing so much work keep in mind i still work in the meat dept that has 4 employees and increably
busy he says no so i say well im not working in the deli anymore oh we'll write u up i said fine i really don,t care hoping to get fired to get unemployment but they didn,t i ended up not showing one day during the busy holiday season. This is not the only company that is like this they all are and from now on im not going to do a good job because you wont get rewarded for it they'll give you more to do or cut your hours. working for bjs and my current job have really changed my outlook on life fuck everyone dont trust anyone and steal from them as much as you can to make up for the shit paycheck you get for busting your ass all week.
Worked there over 15 years can tell you the place started out being run like a family everyone helping out everyone else ..everyone use to hang out after work with each other even went on vacations with each other then slowly it turned into a place where everyone is out for themselves backstabbing

MONKEY WRENCH

others ..i wasn't into that kind of stuff i liked to walk into work do my job and leave but that wasn't enough for them in the end..i went from having 16 co workers in a "zone" to 4 with 2 of them hardly speaking english..one by one i watched all my co workers get fired for no reason other then greed ..the daytime crew wouldn't lift a finger to help on the floor and managers forget it their in their office looking at the menu for their break..now they just look for anyone to fill a spot part time hope they last the month and refill them. just as long as the people at the top get their almighty dollar

Club 113 in Plymouth MA has a gossip group that the GM has up in her office hrs upon hrs. All they do is gossip and shit talk about who they like and don't like. The GM is the laziest piece of shit she does nothing except yell at people and she pretends she knows how things run in each department but has no clue oh and at 1200 she goes around with 6 other managers to fill box bins cause thats a tough job. That club treats good employees like shit unless they kiss the bosses ass. The payroll is a joke and they pull people from every department to help in the deli and then ask all the departments that had their help pulled why things did't get done

Club 67 is currently a mess also. Freezer food is being left out for hours while it is packed out. Dairy is the same. Wanna buy produce, it sat near the dumpster for most of the night. One guy that seems to have been working there forever does nothing but trash talks everyone that is not standing there. One guy works very hard all day but everyone trash talks him like he does nothing. One game seems to happen to everyone. They pay you less than they should and then you have to fight to get the rest. I have heard two people talking about this. Sometimes

MONKEY WRENCH

you get a raise, and it never appears. If you complain, you vanish into the unemployment void. Something needs to change in the company and fast. It looks like this company has been doing this at every store for years by the look at the comments here.

I was hired in 113 as a meat cutter and what I saw in 8 weeks made me head spin, As an experienced professional in the retail food service industry for over 20 years, I have experience as a manager and hourly worker.At 113 I witnessed everything from improper sanitation to ridiculously poor product storage and rotation.Everyone including the perishable manager refused to rotate product when stocking display cases. When questioned about this their reply was "it's ok , it will sell, it's busy". Ready to cook chickens were stored in the cutting room along with coarse ground hamburger trim. Both items were dangerously out of safe product storage temperatures. Daily cleanup routines did not include applying sanitizer as part of the 3 step cleaning process until I mentioned it to my department head. An improperly functioning rotisserie oven was used unsafely for a week before I brought it to the deli manager's attention. His response was that "it won't blow up...actually one did blow up in another club but it will be fine.." My department head was only visible working in the department an average of maybe an hour or two a day. The rest of her work day was spent chatting with the GM and other "managers" or hiding out in her "office" doing "paperwork". I have never seen such a blatant disregard for responsibility in all my years of work. In eight weeks of work I only saw my GM twice and the second time, I had to introduce myself because she didn't even know who I was! The inner circle of management covers each others' backs, resulting in nobody doing any work except the team *members. Some team! For the record, I was terminated prior to my orientation period, so some may call me disgruntled. But honestly, my release was probably the best thing to happen to me as I could not abide by the work ethic of slacker management and the clear cut abuses I saw!*

Club 028 again. We lost [through firing] another manager. That makes three in the span of a year! First the meat manager, then an overnight manager, and now the bakery manager.
And speaking of managers who are now Specialists, have any clubs seen their photos removed from the walls? I looked up one day and saw the fired overnight manager's picture removed. And along with his, the remaining overnight manager's picture as well. Our Sr. Merch told us nothing changed except they are now called Specialists and have to clock in and out. Apparently, you are only a true manager if you are salaried and don't punch in or out.

Regarding the changes to vacation and sick time, I haven't seen any information about it. We still have the same handbooks from a couple of years ago. Where can I find the updates?

Club 028 again.

[quote]So can other overnight crew members post how they work during the night?[quote]

Grab something to eat and drink; this is going to be a long post. This is Part 1.

I was told at one large club the managers, now specialists,

MONKEY WRENCH

came in at 10, and the ticketers come in at 11. The truck[s] come later due to a noise ordinance. A driver unloaded the truck with the Hyster, and drivers carred away the pallets with reach trucks. Each zone had enough help. Each ticketer worked 2-3 aisles. The ticketers packed out, and everyone, including the managers were at the time clock or left at 7am.

I don't know who made the droplists for them.

At our club, a small one, the GM used to make the droplists. If there was none, the managers dropped what they felt was needed. Our new Senior Merchant began making the droplists for the club, and still did after the GM transferred. If there was no droplist, the managers dropped what they felt was needed.

Dropping what was needed could sometimes kill a ticketer. Every zone used to have 2-3 people until the budget got tight and people started getting let go for such things as pallet alignment and performance [still working long past your scheduled time]. We have no recovery team, the ticketers recover and pack out. If you know how to drive a forklift, you can drop your own stuff and pack it out. But a ticketer who didn't know how to drive a forklift usually did the recovery for you.

OK, after the firings, every zone, except Non-Food, was reduced to one person per zone. Managers would drop 30 pallets or more in Food. The one ticketer would have to fend for himself and hope he could finish on time. Food requires much hand stacking, and often recreating entire pallets by hand, such as Carnation, Magnolia, Domino Sugar, 100 lb. rice, ravioli, etc. The real mine field was in the Back 40 where the dog food, cat food, paper items, juice, water, and trash bags are. Managers

MONKEY WRENCH

would drop 60-70 pallets, including the water, on one ticketer! Full-time or part-time, the ticketer had to knock out all the pallets on time.

Before the firings, if scheduling allowed for two people in Food or the Back 40, they would finish early and go help out in other zones. That was good teamwork. After the firings, if a ticketer finished early, he or she would go help out in other zones.

Club 028 again.

This is Part 2.

Knowing how to drive a forklift is a plus because you don't have to worry about a manager overdropping. But you still have to do your own recovery, packing, and booming up. If a manager sees you are very good on a lift, you will be made to do your recovery, help unload the truck, drop your own stuff, pack it out, boom up any leftovers, and help boom up the truck.

If you are OK on a lift, then you may or may not have to drop your own stuff, pack it out, and boom up any leftovers. The specialist might drop for you, but then you are at his mercy.

Our new Food Specialist is a transfer. He played possum on us by dropping 20 or less pallets at first. Once he saw how fast some of us worked [you learn to work fast after you become the only ticketer in your zone], he began to drop heavy. But that was nothing. He would check on you every now and then to see how many pallets you killed. If you killed a lot, he would drop more. If you did your own drops, he would either drop more, or have you drop more. Our Non-Food Specialist had to tell him to

MONKEY WRENCH

ease up. That was the night he overdropped [52 pallets] on the Food Lead, and wound up helping him pack them out. Other pallets, he boomed up, as the merchandise on the sales floor was enough to make it through the next business day.

The man reminds me of our Merch, he loves to work! Both of them came from Million Dollar Clubs, so huge pallet drops and multiple trucks are what they are used to. But that only works if there is enough help. The Merch loves to drop heavy. The only time he doesn't drop heavy is if he is not feeling well. His droplists are smaller then too. And he will recover and pack out if he has to do it. The Merch moves like lightning! The Food Specialist killed over 40 pallets one night he was forced to work the Back 40! He is slow, but he is steady. He had the Food Lead recover for him before sending him to work the freezer. Our GM loves to work too. He will gladly get on a lift and do whatever is needed, from dropping to doing a reset. I used to call him a fireman because the RM had him travel from club to club as a GMIT to put out fires, and/or cover senior management vacations.

The GM implemented a sign program so all ticketer would know how to do signs, but it fell apart after it became nearly impossible to find a Symbol gun. Every now and then we get lucky and have both a Food and Non-Food Symbol for use. Other times, there is one Symbol, no Symbol, or we have to wait until a true manager [not a specialist] arrives with a master key and locates one. If there is no Symbol before our shift is done, we don't hang around once we get one. Hanging around after your shift earns you more work, often times, other peoples work. I remember in my green [naive] days, if my previous GM saw me after my scheduled time, he would have me recover

MONKEY WRENCH

the dairy and do other stuff as ways to motivate me to get off the clock.

Does anyone who worked or still works overnight have any anecdotes they would like to share?

Chapter Eight: Dial 911

The weekend is one of the worst days of the week to have to run an entire club by yourself whether you are a salaried daytime manager, or overnight specialist who is on the clock. It's par for the course for day managers thanks to the mass culling in January 2016. As far as Overnight Specialists, that practice had been going on for decades regardless of the situation.

September 10, 2017, the Florida Keys were devastated by Hurricane Irma. Irma then began a northbound path through Miami, Fort Lauderdale, and other surrounding cities before taking a detour west to Naples. It continued north and its winds left cities, such as Jacksonville flooded. By the time she left Florida, she was going into Georgia as a tropical depression.

This particular year, FEMA (Federal Emergency Management Agency) did something unprecedented for Florida residents-it gave them FREE money for their losses. But not just any FREE money, it came in the form of food stamps through D-SNAP (Disaster Supplemental Assistance Program). Thousands of residents formed long lines to apply for the benefits. Some received hundreds of dollars, and there were instances of people receiving a thousand dollars loaded onto benefits cards.

DIAL 911

Income was not a factor, only being affected.

Needless to say, Floridians descended upon retail establishments en masse. They bought items they would have never purchased with their own funds whether earned or government-provided. Each day, shelves were demolished as if the hurricane were on its way instead of long gone! In charge of the night crew of one location, was a 24 year-old, recently promoted Overnight Specialist. It was a Friday night, he faced at least two truck deliveries, and had no overnight receiver to assist him. That was daunting enough, but expected because that was what he signed up for when he took the position. However, that particular night, he shouldn't have been there.

His father-in-law passed away, so his wife and child were out of town for the funeral. That was bad enough, but it got worse. He found out a day or so later, his grandmother passed away.

BJ's allows paid bereavement time. After bereavement time ends, an employee may take more time, but it will be on their own time: personal, vacation, or unpaid. The guy needed time away for these back-to-back personal events in his life. The General Manager didn't want to hear any of it, and told him there was nobody else to cover the shift. One overnight specialist was on vacation. The other one was off, and about to go on vacation too.

Our bodies and minds are connected in ways most do not understand. And that night, the effects of that young man's burdened mind affected his body in one of the worst ways possible. He stepped off his forklift, and collapsed at end of an aisle.

DIAL 911

Three former Overnight Specialists worked that night. There was a fourth, but he worked during the day. Four former Overnight Specialists working in the same building speaks volumes about the position. One of them was in pain from an injury he sustained when and older Overnight Specialist ran into him with a forklift while he carried a stack of cardboard. So he had an ice pack, and was on his way home. When he went to tell the overnight specialist he was leaving, he found him on the floor, clutching his chest, and unable to move or speak!

He told a coworker to dial 911 while he stayed with him. One of the other former specialists saw what was happened, helped the guy into a chair, and wheeled him to the back of the store where the paramedics would come when they arrived.

This was a situation two Overnight Specialists predicted in the past. What would the night crew do if there were only one overnight specialist on duty, and that person fell out or died? We ran a list of ideas by one of them, and he laughed. That night, we tested one of those ideas.

The two former specialists tried to contact the General Manager and the Senior Merchandising Manager, but neither responded. It's hypocritical that senior managers can call or text overnight specialists, and they must respond, but not the other way around. They even dialed the Regional Asset Protection Manager to no avail. That was when one employee put his idea into action, and called a nearby store. Nearly the entire overnight crew was new, except for a couple of employees. He asked for an Overnight Specialist he new when he was a Senior Merchandising Manager before he stepped

DIAL 911

down to an hourly forklift driver, and then got promoted to overnight specialist. He told him the situation, and knew he still had contact with people in high places who could help. He told the employee he would work on it, and to standby. In the meantime, the paramedics came and took the overnight specialist to the hospital. The former Overnight Specialist who found him went along in his vehicle so he could translate, if needed, and to be there until the fallen specialist's family arrived, which were his sister and brother-in-law.

Back at the store, the employee who called the other store made an announcement to inform the overnight crew of what happened. He learned from the best Senior Merchandising Manager in South Florida that communication was key in important situations. He let them know they were alone for the time, and to continue as if they still had management in the building. That meant continue the tasks at hand, and do them no less better than if they were supervised.

Some time later, the very one who told the overnight specialist there was nobody to cover the shift appeared, and he wasn't alone. The General Manager came, along with the Senior Merchandising Manager, and the Overnight Specialist from the other store. The latter stayed and helped run and put away the freight from one of the trucks before he had to go back to his store and help with a second truck delivery it received.

The very thing he and another specialist predicted finally came to fruition. Less than a week later, the young man was back on the job, and working alone again on a Friday night. Exactly one day short of a month later, he came to work, and looked a little out of sorts. He had a long conversation with someone on his

DIAL 911

cell phone, and less than two hours later, he walked out, leaving the store in the hands of the last specialist left-one who'd been with the company for 29 years. A specialist who had been with the company 25 years walked out about three weeks prior, but returned two days later. However, the night after Thanksgiving, which was Black Friday night, he was a no show, and the new specialist called out sick.

Once again, nobody wanted to answer the phone. The overnight crew was left to oversee itself. The Member Service Manager was forced to stay at work well past her shift until another manager could arrive. The Operations Manager had to return to work after being there from 2-9:30, and leaving because of a headache. He stayed until 6 AM, an hour after the Senior Merchanding Manager came in at 5 AM for his regular shift, and not one minute earlier.

This place will kill you, and nobody will give a care about you if it does.

Chapter Nine: Paid In Bananas

It seems that BJ's is adopting a universal raise for club-level employees. As of last year, the company started handing out paltry 25 cent raises to hourly team members. No matter your contributions, that was going to be the new maximum. There are always exceptions, of course. Some team mates received less, few received more. Those on salary receive percent raises and bonuses. This is a slap in the face for many who go above and beyond in their jobs. Many stellar employees cut back on their performance when they received what one of my friends who has been with the company 25+ years, their "yearly insult". How high can your morale be when you go above and beyond, yet receive the same raise as someone who just meets expectations? It totally erodes what you were brought up to believe. And that is to be kind, courteous, work hard, do the best job you can, and you will be rewarded for it.

Sam's Club, and especially Costco, pay their employees much higher starting wages. Even recent German newcomer, Aldi, pays it's cashiers higher stating wages than BJ's. After many years, BJ's tried to get on the bandwagon. In 2015, it raised its minimum hiring wage to $9/hour. Some months later, it raised it again, this time to $10/hour. Why another raise within the same year? It means upper management didn't know what it was

PAID IN BANANAS

doing the first time. As always, there is much ire from employees already in the system who just started to make those hourly rates. BJ's goal was to attract the best talent available. Money was not the way. Just like in the real estate market, it's location, location, location.

People read about, or may had first hand experience with public schools in neighbors with low incomes and high crime rates. It does not take a degree to understand that correlation. The same for fast food restaurants and service companies, such as Taco Bell, Papa John's, Metro PCS, and The Check Cashing Store. And don't think banks are excluded from this. I worked as a teller at several bank locations while with First Union. Locations in urban areas had predominately urban employees, except for management. Locations in suburban areas had employees indicative of that.

So if BJ's wants better talent, it needs to place its locations in better areas. Costco and Sam's Clubs are generally located in middle-class areas or commercial districts.

Regarding pay, BJ's has been sued three times for misclassifying managers to avoid paying overtime wages.[3] And each time, the company admits no wrongdoing. They just pay the money, make a few changes, and then it's monkey business as usual. But as of the time of this writing, a new federal law will soon take effect. December 1, 2016, salaried workers who earn less than $47,476 per year will qualify for overtime wages when they exceed 40 hours a week.

Here is the latest update on that, courtesy of an overnight specialist who was in shock by the news because he wasn't in

PAID IN BANANAS

the know about things. Thankfully, I listen to NPR, and not mainstream media. You will never heard about this on your local news channel. He mentioned some managers at a nearby club received $10,000 raises. I explained the new federal law to him, and he was even more astounded. BJ's risk management team or their financial side of the company, must have done a cost-benefit analysis and found to track and to pay salaried managers overtime for hours worked over 40, would be too costly for the company. They also found that to convert them to hourly would be too much of a hassle along with being costly. So to keep things status quo, just give them the extra money, and that will be the end of it. Pay up big now to avoid paying up even bigger down the road. Many of you are too young to remember the Ford Pinto recall in 1978. But maybe you remember the GM ignition switch cover up in 2007. As always, someone within the company, whether it be executives, or middle management, knows something is wrong, yet figures it will be more costly to fix the problem than to let things play out on their own, and deal with the financial aftermath.[6]

Still, people need vehicles. So no matter which auto company has a scandal, they always bounce back from it. BJ's needs managers to stay late to get the work done, and to not pay extra for it. Each year, each BJ's location conducts its own inventory, usually in conjunction with an outside company, such as RGIS. That week, all managers must work six days. After that, they compensate them with an extra day off down the road. So imagine all of those salaried managers taking home a six-day check. Oh, and inventory last forever because it takes so long to transmit all the numbers to Home Office, and for Home Office to compare them with their numbers, and send back the results. BJ's is way behind on the technology curve. As of the latter part

PAID IN BANANAS

of this year [2016], it just adopted online pay and in-store pickup.

Getting back to inventory night, I remember "fondly" being scheduled from 4 PM-12 AM along with another coworker. It ended up being 4 PM-4 AM! Management thinks people want the hours, but quite frankly, most would rather have their time-at home...in bed.

I don't know about other companies, but BJ's penalizes team members when they "make too much". It's not the employee's fault. Maybe they received the highest raises, learned knew skills for more money, received promotions, or simply stayed with the company for eons. It's hypocritical that those who become upset about those under them making too much money, are those who are senior managers on salary, and receiving bonuses. I don't think they would agree if their bosses told them they made too much money. There is your misplaced blame at work again. Blame the employee instead of the company who instituted the pay structure in 1984, when those same seniors probably never heard of BJ's Wholesale Club. Heck, I only knew about Sam's Club thanks to relatives who had a membership to one in Statesboro, Georgia. I didn't know about Costco or BJ's until 2007.

BJ's does have some amazing benefits and rewards, even if it doesn't match the pay of its rivals: birthday pay, personal day pay, Star of the Month day off with pay, and Star of the Year day off with pay and $300. The $300 used to be in paid as a gift card. But as of 2016, it's included in your pay, and taxed.
There is another way to make a money as an employee, and that is to help the company save money. Makes sense, right? If

PAID IN BANANAS

someone you pay, can show you a way to save a substantial amount of money, they should be rewarded for it. Unlike Star of the Month and Star of the Year, which excludes managers because they choose who wins, management is not exempt from this reward. BJ's called this the E.A.S.Y. [Efficiency, Accuracy, Simplicity & You] program. Now as close to the problems as many hourly employees are, somehow they seem to have no viable solutions to them. Why do I say that? Because every photo in the quarterly BJ's employee magazine shows a mid manager or senior manager happily brandishing a $250 check for a cost saving or efficiency improving idea.

Corrupt cops with gold badges....

Do you really think law enforcement reports ALL the cocaine and money seized in a major drug bust? There are always *justifications* for taking more than you are making. See Chapter Nine.

Pay is always a hot topic, which is the reason people feel uncomfortable discussing it. How about this for funny. When people think they are paid too little, they won't tell you what they make. When they think they are paid too much, they definitely won't tell you what they make!

I have worked for BJ's for over three years now and have about had my fill after seeing my W2. I can't believe the duties to perform as a Deli Supervisor in a deli that pulls in over 10 thousand a week in a slow week and over 13 in the summer and holidays. I work 6 days a week and one of those days is sunday open to close. I made 23,000+ this year and I am now furious to find out that this position only gets one raise upto 50

PAID IN BANANAS

cents a year. I work my but off for this company and I have since day one. Not only to better the company but to better myself. I do whatever they tell me and everyone under me in my department calls out at least once a week making it nearly impossible to get work done. I however have only used two days sick time in the past year for oral surgery. I consider myself a model employee that take my job as if it was my own business. Why? because I have pride in my own work. They say they base pay on surrounding stores, all of those stores do not do half the work it takes to do what we do to keep the store running. They have people in thier headquarters doing the ordering. Not taking a week off for the holidays when I worked 2 months straight with one day off. They have work areas built around safety and make it so much eaiser for sanitation. and finally, they have the payroll. And your welcome for the 89 1/2 hours I worked to help rebuild all the steel in the building. Or the fact that for the first time since my family members passed away I couldn't visit my grandparents grave this Christmas season because I was counted on as the Deli Supervisor to make it through the holiday season with only 3 other employees in the department. Now tell me I am not good enough for a raise. That is what working at BJ's means to me this January while the company get's richer and richer and we get poorer and poorer. Thank you BJ's for the holiday bonus I worked so hard for this season.

They need to eliminate Bonuses for coming in under budgeted payroll. All that leads to is inefficiency and poor moral. The hourly workers are not stupid. And enough with this 30 hour full time and 37.5 hour full time. Confusing as hell. Cant tell you how many people thought they were being hired at 40 hour full, then get told no its really only 30 hour. Some deceptive hiring

PAID IN BANANAS

practices by some HR

We are all working for the same company,yet the North gets time and a half for Sundays the Southern stores do not.Full time up North is 37.5 hours in the South they tell you its 30-37.5 and give you 30.Its time that all clubs get the same standards,

Speaking of ticketers. Does anyone know if a person is offered an overnight supervisor or team lead postion if he/she has to accept raise amount offered, or can the person ask for more?

All HO has to do is plug in some info, and a number [dollar amount] comes up.

The same goes for overnight specialists. Does one have to accept what's offered? Has anyone asked for more money for the promotion, and got it?

well, i think the reclassification and switch to hourly sucks for us overnight managers. we have schedules in our club already and we are losing days...money out of my pocket now...to those in the clubs whose gm isn't changing thier ways congrats, you are the ones who will benefit the most. the original perks to taking a promotion was no punching in/out, direct deposit, and salary. now all employees get direct deposit, i have to punch in/out and my pay is directly related to my hours....which have been cut :(what is the perks now? bonuses gone and all....GLORIFIED TICKETERS...ahem i mean TICKETER SPECIALIST lol
Maybe they were with bjs way before all this bullshit started to happend. If life is about options and choices where were their option to vote on this for the choice to be made. Remember bjs

PAID IN BANANAS

doesnt pay the people the customers pay the people bjs is just the middle man. Higher wages equals happier employees wich means they are nicer to customers which drive up sales. (cough cough) Costco.......

How about paying dividends of $643,000,000.00 to new owners and upper management? To above anonymous: You may see how payroll budget gets crunched down and how some people don't get their hours or how new hires are part timers in your club. If you see that at club level and the difference is small change but adds up to a big chunk of cash. Why wouldn't anyone expect that at corporate level they wouldn't have plans to downgrade other expenses i.e. healthcare, vacation, sick time, personal days. I see in my club raises this year where capped at 25 cents per hour and they changed the standards without informing us. So rather than just cap the raises and let us get fair reviews they beat us up on the reviews to justify the 25 cent raise. Now I see in the system there is a new review form, one with FIRST as an acyronym (sp?), I doubt that many will see the new form before thier review time and once again they will have changed the standards without inform us. You really can't satisfy this master because we are told we are a team but get graded as individuals. Basically BJ's Wholesale Club is a taker not a giver in fairness. When you take a stand on anything you had better have a lawyer standing with you.

i have worked at bj's since graduating high school last year, and i have been treated rather badly. after the schedule is posted i am constantly asked to switch my days off and my hours as well. i am a cashier, but they have me doing lp-front door and i told them i had no interest in anything but cashiering, they

PAID IN BANANAS

wouldnt take no for an answer, and being im flexible they take advantage of me.

the fls's all take turns calling out and flipping other peoples schedules, i think this is unfair. i brought this up to my manager, and she told me that they appreciate my flexibility, but what about my days off that i would like to enjoy? i always dread answering the phone when they call me. aking me to work in the food court when someone calls out. i need the money because i would like to move out, and i wouldnt mind working extra hours, but they always switch me around so i get inconvenienced and then i get 37.5 hours. does this happen at other bj's? i never call out, and i try to be helpful to my managers and co-workers, but i would like some extra incentive for my flexibility. and a food court voucher is not going to be the answer. sorry for the the long post.

me

E: me said....
Welcome to the world of BJ'S
A couple of questions

1. When you filled out your application, what did you write down for availability?
2. Become an FLS,learn Member Services and you can make more $$$ with LESS grief, and less chance of write-ups
3. By showing initiative (which you are currently doing), you could possibly move into Management, make even more $$$ than you EVER COULD being a cashier.
JUST REMEMBER THIS- We can't control everything that happens

PAID IN BANANAS

to us, BUT... we can control how we respond to what happen to us.

When I was offered this job, I was guaranteed 40 hours. Now because of cuts I am only getting 30. With lunch I'm now only getting 27. WTF? How am I supposed to survive on that. They don't care about us in the least. I already took a huge pay cut coming here and now I'm about to loose my home. Thanks for the lies BJ's. When I asked about my house being cut, My manager asked if I was turning in my resignation. Where is the compassion? The managers are all a joke, over paid and hypocrites. They are salary, with much less to worry about. I'm so over qualified for this job.

Three are plenty of opportunities that are to be had at BJ's. I started out in the deli deptartment making $7.00/per hr(Sept 06) I signed up for the meat department apprentice & as of now i have more than double my starting rate from 2 years ago.

BJ's has treated me very good, & i give them the same in return. It's not hard to acheive at BJ's, especially if you do your job well & not call out every week.

The only problem with being promoted from within is those hired from the outside are hired in making more money then those promoted from within. They should take your BJ's experience into account when being promoted.

I find it hard to believe that $20.00 per hour positions exist at BJS. I have been trained in multiple departments, which IMO, would make me very valuable. I do not make $20.00 per hour, far from it.

PAID IN BANANAS

Those figures spoken about in the previous blog are inaccurate at best.

The average rate of pay at Costco is $16/hr. I wish they would locate a store in this area.

I am a former Personnel Manager, trust me, those numbers are correct. If a Meat cutter was hired with an experience rate, got good reviews and has been in the position for awhile, he/she could be making $20 an hour easily.

"How about the produce guy who cant get his truck off the receiving dock because their is so much crap on it."

The produce specialists are the most overpayed employees, by far. They are $20+/hr stockers that will soon be eliminated. They perform 2 hours of work on a busy day at best. An overhaul of the produce speacialist is long overdue. Our Produce Spec thinks she is the almighty, but she'll be gone soon enough.

I totally agree that produce specialist are overpaid, but the positon is needed specailly in the busier clubs. When BJ's took over the produce Dept, they made a bad decision to pay the produce specialist so much money. They should have made it a Mid manager position. Currently if a produce specialist works 40 hours a week, including Sunday, they can make more money then a mid manager. But they again, it's the same with all the perishable depts. Perishable Managers, meat cutters,

PAID IN BANANAS

bakers, produce specialist are all overpaid if you ask me. Unfortunalty that's the way retail works.

BJ's should delete the Produce Specialist position($16-$24/hr) and replace them with a simple produce lead position which could make $10-$12 hr.

In our club, the produce employee who make $7 per hour, does more than that shithead Specialist, Steph.

Club 028 again.

Like Batman, I've worked days and nights. Regarding EBT, we didn't allow them at SCO. EBT members had to use regular lanes. As far as I remember, there were no non member surcharges assessed to them. Believe me, EBT users scrutinized their receipts as did CC, debit, check, and cash users. So if they saw a surcharge, they would have immediately spoke up.

Back to the lawsuit, which is so much fun to talk about. Our GM finally got tired of babysitting us every Saturday night from 10pm until 12am. According to him, he could not "afford" to pay the specialists from 10pm until 12am. He would drive and drop, and drop, and drop, and drop out of sheer boredom, or possibly frustration. The Merch had a droplist, but the GM would just go by the "what's needed" method. So then the specialists would arrive, tell the GM about the droplist he already knew about, and then drop on top of the "what's needed".
One Saturday night, the GM took the night off. He tried to get a mid manager to cover from 10pm until 12am. Every one of

PAID IN BANANAS

them refused, and stood on some corporate rule about staying until 12am. That night, we all had to come in at midnight. And to make matters worse, it was the night/morning of Daylight Savings Time.

Some TMs requested to come in at 12am from a while back because of their second jobs. Others just couldn't make it at 10pm because they liked to sleep late. That's all fine and dandy.

But this next thing wasn't fine and dandy. The next week, without so much as a brief meeting, the GM changed overnight TM's schedule to 12-6 or 12-8 just for Saturday night going into Sunday morning. The 10pm people feel that is very unfair. But it seems to be a done deal.

Reply

Don't forget, the lawyers get 33% of the total.

Under the settlement, approximately 1,500 current and former Mid Managers employed by BJ's since November 2007 will be entitled to make claims to share in the recovery, based on the number of weeks they were employed by the company.

There is NO WAY anyone will be getting ALL the overtime they would be entitled to.

Don't think it's very fair that it's being divided evenly. Not all mids put in the same amount of hours. You can write in what you "think" your owed, but you need to provide proof. Who really kept track of hours they worked over the course of those

PAID IN BANANAS

particular five years?

If one did on average 10 hours overtime a week (and most I know did), that's 40 hours a month. So, at least a weeks pay for every month you were a salaried mid. Nice chunk eh? Not gonna happen.

The company will start to see what mids do when were cramming X amount of work into Y amount of time. If a salaried mid took till 10 or 11 am to get things perfect, well that's their time. Get done early, good for you. Now, your not done? Sorry, no OT... see ya later.

Why do you think there are so many Overnight Manager Positions listed on BJ's Employment site......

Who wants to work 70 plus hours a week overnight vs 45 hours a week dayside...... for a $75.00 a week shift differential..... wow, that is $3.00 per hour, not even minimum wage, to deal with BS
from dayside management and senior merchandise managers

What you have are Senior Merchandise Managers make unrealistic demands on the Overnight Managers....
dayside is a cakewalk compared to overnight

Dayside who never did overnights should spend 2 weeks working the overnight managers schedual to get an understanding of what happens when they are sleeping
Here it is. Not in a nut shell but with first hand experience. This suit was brought on by overnight managers. These managers are responsible for the duties to be performed by the

PAID IN BANANAS

associates. With short staffing of associates the managers become responsible to complete the job. Day after day there are not enough hands to complete the jobs. Managers are then doing the jobs of the associates.

This suit started 2 years ago. I have worked there for 8 years. Staff has been cut back every one of these years. Also bring to this that business has grown over these years. What was the solution? Like I said before, make managers do more associate work. Push came to shove and salaried managers are now performing the same duties as associates. Work that is not exempt from wage and hour laws.

My prediction is that this settlement will change the way retail management plans for growth. Bottom line growth will begin to be in line with operating costs, not bottom line desires. End does not justify the means anymore. Run your company better, not just pressure to make the buck.

At BJ's there is a lucrative bonus plan for upper store management. Meet these goals and you are on your way up with cash in your pocket. This suit puts a dent into that logic. Time to pay the people to what they are doing and for management to do a better job of managing.

I speak from nearly 30 years of retail. Mostly in management. I had seen this thing coming and got out of management for the above reasons. I do my job as an associate and go home. You got my 40 hours. You want more? Pay me overtime or find someone else to do my job.
That is what the entire lawsuit was/is about. Overnight, bakery, and LP managers will be paid overtime starting Jan. 17th. We

PAID IN BANANAS

will not be called managers anymore. Now we are "Specialists".

Nothing else changes except we now punch in/out, get overtime pay, lose bonus, and change position title.

I work around 60 hours a week. When the seniors come in at 6:00am and want to change the entire store around, I have to do it. That means I work 11-12 hours a day. I can not wait until Jan. 17th. Overtime!!

We have a saying at our store:

"Overnight managers are just glorified ticketers."

Chapter Ten: Monkey Hustle

"The Monkey Hustle" was an old school comedy from the the blaxplotation era. It was about the daily hustle of getting over on those who were getting over on others. You dig?

I remember a long time ago, someone told me about a CSM who walked out with $30,000 cash at the end of the night. Then there were the stories about two senior managers were terminated for outright theft, and one from coupon fraud theft...all at the same location!

A manager who came up quickly from being a recovery clerk to being a mid-manager, thanks to him looking just like Hulk Hogan and Goldberg [learn about the Beauty Myth, Halo Effect, or studies that people with good genetics have personal and professional advantages over those who do not], eventually became a MSM. He had a girlfriend with expensive tastes. One day, her tastes led him to buy four new tires for her car, and he committed coupon fraud to pay for them. Years later, another MSM was walking around the same club, and eating food. When asked if he had a receipt, he couldn't produce one. He got what I call The 4th of July Special, meaning he got fired. The last MSM loaded on the back of his truck, a meat department oven that was designated for salvage.

MONKEY HUSTLE

This particular location was known for having the most management attrition in the region since it opened in 2008. However, for some reason, nobody in upper management seemed to notice. And nobody in middle management seemed to do anything about it.

A manager who came up quickly from being a recovery clerk to being a mid-manager, thanks to him looking just like Hulk Hogan and Goldberg [learn about the Beauty Myth, Halo Effect, or studies that people with good genetics have personal and professional advantages over those who do not], eventually became a MSM. He had a girlfriend with expensive tastes. One day, her tastes led him to buy four new tires for her car, and he committed coupon fraud to pay for them. Years later, another MSM was walking around the same club, and eating food. When asked if he had a receipt, he couldn't produce one. He got what I call The 4th of July Special, meaning he got fired. The last MSM loaded on the back of his truck, a meat department oven that was designated for salvage.

The MSM had some issue with the daytime recevier, a headstrong lesbian who was terrific at her forklift job, and it came back to haunt him. She was the very one who reported him, and he was promptly suspended. Management suspension during an "investigation" means termination 100 percent of the time. I've only seen hourly employees survive suspensions, and that was because the managers who reported them did not have all their ducks in a row.

Once you become a BJ's mangager, you are given the coveted gold badge. The way I see them, many managers become

MONKEY HUSTLE

"corrupt cops with gold badges". They will not go against one another, even if one of them makes the wrong call on something. We had a forced meeting once, and the silverback gorilla of the overnight specialists, flat out told us they would not go against one another. Corruption and kangaroo courts run rampant at BJ's. I remember being the defendent in a kangaroo court. I felt like telling the Senior Merchant and the new Overnight Food Specialist something from "Transformers: The Movie". The last surviving member of a planet of robots said to the judge and jury, a five-faced, robot monstrosity with tentacles, "Spare me this mockery of justice!" The robot pronounced him "Innocent" right before dropping him from a plank into a pool of hungry robot sharks. I refused to sign the not write up write up, known as a Note to File, and wrote how I felt. The next time I talked to the Senior Merchant, he asked me what a kangaroo court was. I told you, just because they are managers, doesn't make them smart.

So let us take a look at how managers and hourly employees get over on their employer, on other team members, and how some creatively maintain the status quo. BJ's is full of weasels. You will see the acroynm SOM and SOY used, which mean Star of the Month and Star of the Year. Both of which are either granted on merit or favortism, which is universal.

Managers CAN get WRITTEN UP,and TERMINATED just like hourly employees.

DOCUMENT EVERYTHING.... DAY,DATE,TIME,PLACE, INFRACTION, ETC.

When you can prove your point with 100% accuracy, do you

MONKEY HUSTLE

honestly think most managers remember detail like that. Keep the notebook out of sight and don't tell a soul what you are writing down. The brown nosers and pets might rat you out if they knew what you were doing...

what can an employee do about internal theft when everyone looks the other way? my meat manager chomps down on cheese, salami, sandwiches, chickens, wings and just about anything open, but threatens to fire anyone else on the spot if they are caught, but then offers them cheese and salami 20 minutes later. the second in command is the same. i've approached countless managers and supervisors with this problem including regionals. but it keeps happening. has anyone succeeded in getting this situation resolved? morale is down through the ground because of these idiotic managers roaming around in the company. help!

Have you spoken with the regional Loss Prevention Manager? As a former LP, that is considered theft, but you need to completely document ALL incidents (ex: on 4-29-10 @ 10:45 AM, Joe Smith, Meat Manager @ Club # 000 opened a roll of salami, sliced a 1/2 lb and took it in his office, where he began eating it without paying for it). Once you get 3 or more documented incidents, call in the Regional LP and let the manager squirm.....

*Managers are now chosen by if they are in the Gm's little click. Take **Hen Schw** for instance, laziest person on earth then they make him Operations Manager. While all Gm's were in Florida, **Hen** called a couple of Clubs to gossip about what was confided to him by higher ups about the Gm at the south Philly Club Al would be fired when they get back from Florida which*

MONKEY HUSTLE

still hasn't happened yet. Then you have a female Gm who while she was a Member Service manager committed coupon fraud time and time again and was caught at it and was caught doing rewards fraud but because she is in the click made GM.

Club 156
There is too much that happens to mention, from the top to down. Meat manager abuse of 1800# to get another manager fired because that manager issued a write up to his girlfriend how's that? That's three he called on. Of course they must think that's ok. Because the whole club now knows about it. The 1800# number was taken down. Was it taken down in other clubs? Is this their way of keeping business in house so they call it!

I noticed yesterday that the 800# was replaced and put on the wall near the closet behind the maintence cart. I am so frustrated and angry and grossly dissapointed in the level of unprofessionalism at the store. Ed just came in to our store last week and question many of the employees about pros and cons and asked everyone what they would do if they were the GM. I just hope that it gets better.

Its a favoritism thing. At our club, a part timer who is late a great deal, texts on his cell phone during work, etc got SOY but because he is a butt kisser, he gets on avg 45-50 hours a week, gets any extra shifts available with out Personnel even letting anybody else know they are available, he gets SOY over people who have gone far and above their job descriptions, work hard, never late and who bust their asses every single day and never get any recognition. Its mostly seems to be about color too, as in if your not african American you dont really

MONKEY HUSTLE

stand a chance of any recognition.

*I have worked for Bjs for 19 years now and working for CLUB 033 has been an good experience minus the corruption going on in member services with employees such as **JIR HAI** that scans her membership card so she can get more rewards or when she pockets stuff from lost and found. NO one in the stores will say anything because **JIR HAI** sucks up to all the managers asses even though Corporate has told the store to fire her on 3 separate occasions, but **JIR** can't get fired because she is **Deb** little bitch!!!!! Not to mention that **JIR** was fired from her other job for stealing and now she has been stealing from this job for years and everyone at Club 033 has had enough. After checking what she spent last year which was over $25,000 which is impossible to spend that much because she doesn't even make that much a year and there is no way someone spends that much without committing some type of fraudulent purchases. Besides **JIR HAI** there is also another thief that stole thousands from the cash office and uses fraudulent coupons such as taking the $5 water jug vouchers and paying for merchandise, but she won't get fired because she is having an affair with the GM. Which is not fair for any of the employees because the management team have their own little circle that have each others backs and that's all they care about. This has been my store for 19 years and I care for my store because we are all here to prosper and make the Club money not here to scan our memberships for customers so I can get more rewards or steal from the cash office and do whatever I want because I'm sleeping with the GM.*

I remember the days when...

MONKEY HUSTLE

1. A GM from Mays Landing spent more time hitting golf balls at a local Country Club then in his own building. Everybody knew about it, and yet nothing was done about it.

2. A Operations Manager from Hamilton would forge customers initials on invoices for recently purchased tires just to pass an audit.

3. How SELECT clubs EXCEEDED allowable inventory loss and it was " worked out "

4. Paperwork for transfers to other clubs got 'LOST'

There are too many incidents to list...

Hey Corporate...
Create a site, and post it here so that you can speak with former employees. I would love to speak with them

Chapter Eleven: Monkeying Around

Being in close proximity to each other so often, leads up to the inevitability that employees are bound to hook up, get into relationships, or get married to each other. However, you must go about it the right way-the smart way. But we know that when it comes to matters of the heart, the mind shuts down. When that happens, job performance is affected, bad decisions are made, and in the end, someone is going to get transferred for it, or fired.

The first BJ's where I first worked, the Personnel Manager who was 26 or 27, had a 19 year-old cashier as her boyfriend. Managers and specialists can date hourly employees, but they cannot be closely tied to each other in such a way that may cause preferential treatment.

Our CSM was 28-29, and was the cashier's direct manager. She was friends with the PM, and the PM's sister, who was a FLS. Alright, now you get the picture.

Everyone knew the kid was taking advantage of his girlfriend. He was what you would call, a scrub. Pants hanging down, no shoelaces, which he paid for one day when the CSM made him go push carts as his punishment, drove his girlfriend's car when

MONKEYING AROUND

he got off work, or it was his day off, and came to pick her up late after she finished work. He also got her to give him money. She was wrapped around his finger, and each week, the kid had 39-40 hours, thanks to her. All of this eventually became too much for her, and she would have panic attacks. Poor thing-she was a size 0, her sister was a size 1. After management could no longer tolerate the way he affected her and her job, they fired him. Shortly thereafter, she and her sister picked up stakes, and moved away.

Here are some more relationships that I found out about at the next location I worked. The first was between an Overnight Specialist and a Computer Room team member. Each morning, he would pretend to recover the printer ink at exactly the same time she would enter the building and walk down a back aisle that led there. They would talk until she had to clock in for work. During a meeting, as she sat, he stood right behind her. As I said, matters of the heart, shut down the mind. She was married to a huge guy. It was evident because her son who worked in the bakery was huge. He later became a Bakery Manager after his mother got the 4th of July Special for insubordination. The specialist caved under too many changes at work, and transferred. I came to learn, he was the only reason she was still there. Some time ago, she wanted to quit, but he talked to her, and one thing led to another. With him gone, she began slacking at her job. One day, she cursed out her direct manager, a newly transferred and trained RICM who was a high riser within the company thanks to her looks, bad attitude, and anal attention to detail, but mostly her looks. It became known that she monkeyed around with a couple of GMs, which led to some fast promotions from FLS to Deli Supervisor to CSM to RICM to PM to OPS/AMO. Her husband

MONKEYING AROUND

was also a high riser. They were opposites, but had the same goal, to become senior managers. They left the company after attaining their goals.

Within that same location, the Senior Merchant was seeing the Cash Office Supervisor. She was one of the most beautiful young women there. They hid it as best as they could, but once she became pregnant, and came to work driving his late model Mercedes-Benz SUV, everyone knew-including the GM, and he was livid. The GM must've spoken with the Regional Manager because the Senior Merchant was banished to a club farther north with the GM's former rival, a former GMIT who was a high riser from Xtra and Albertsons. He got his act together after that, and became one of the best managers in the region. Later, he was rewarded with his own club. I don't know if he ever married the Cash Office Supervisor as he told her he would, or if they are still together.

Personally, I think one of the worst endings was when upper management led a sting operation against a GM and a Bakery Manager, both who were at the same location. You guessed it, the one opened in 2008 with the highest management turnover in the region.

The GM was a married man, and involved with the Bakery Manager much younger than him. Regional management must have somehow caught onto this, and launched a sting operation using an OPS and a CSM. Later, the Bakery Manager transferred to another location, and became a MARM. After the sting was complete, the GM and MARM got the 4th of July Special. A few months later, the GM passed away. Some say it was a drug overdose. But I think it could've been from

MONKEYING AROUND

being unemployed. Often, the activity of employment is the only thing that keeps people going. Ever wonder why some senior citizens are door greeters, bag groceries, or volunteer at events and charities? Yes, some need the money to supplement their fixed incomes, but it is mainly to avoid vegetating at home.

Well, those were the relationships I witnessed. Now read the blog relationship recollections.

I see everyone has issues at thier club. Its so many politics at my store. I am quiet and hardly noticed at my club but I see and hear everything. I work at club 150 and I see it everyday. We have this amazon as our HR manager and one night I was working in the gas station and seen her boyfriend with his car in the tire center, doing his brakes. Most of our managers are married and its an awful lot of affairs going on. The black girls that work the front are so ..... Managers hire friends and let them do whatever. I been there almost 3 years and thier friends get hired and get better schedules than me,

At BJ's Wholesale, when first hired you receive a handbook of rules, regulations and policy of what the company demands. Some of the policies are no favorites... treat all people equal and fair... And no sexual relations between managers and the basic worker. Well that does not apply at Club 167 because you have a manager named **Mi Hen** *whom is dating a girl named* **Jil***. Not only are they dating, but living together. The humorous element to this all is that she sleeps around with majority of the guys at this particular club. On the other hand Mike should be punished for violating the BJ's handbook.*

I use to work at BJs 167 awhile ago. People complaining about

MONKEYING AROUND

all this issues have a right to, but realize this much... Nothing will be done to these managers. When I was working there Wendy B was caught in the L.P. Office with this night worker Ron. Were they doing the dirty? No one knows. But from what I was told by numerous people they came out of that room looking very suspicious. Some how I was canned for that incident amongst other things. I never saw eye to eye with S. Sowers. The point that I am making is that Wendy should have been fired too.

[quote]I'm not doubting that the guy pitches in and helps out but doing someone elses job? Is that the criteria to be SOY? So what your standard to be SOM or SOY is to do everyone else's job in the club?? That can't be right? Some would say the guy is an ass kisser. So is that the criteria?[end quote]

Club 028 again,

We two young ladies who transferred from our Zone 1 VP's store, one drove a forklift, the other came from the gas station. Both came to the overnight shift. Neither of them kissed @$$. They worked the crap out of the forklift TM [even while her hand was hurt], while the other TM got "cozy" with the Non-Food Manager. The gas station TM initiated lots of self-proposed resets and racked up countless of hours of OT with the Non-Food Manager. She was the first overnight TM in years to get SOM.

The forklift TM got her work done and left on time. Shortly thereafter, she went to days. I warned her that once the day shift knew how good and efficient she was, she would end up everywhere. I was right. They scheduled her for produce,

MONKEYING AROUND

DVDs, and cashier for her first week on day shift. She then did FLS, liquor store, Front Door LP, helped drop merchandise not on the floor, and filled in for the Receiving forklift driver doing the water, paper, Burris, and candy trucks while he was on vacation. OK, here is the kicker. She NEVER once received SOM. One night, she broke down at the Front Door LP because no one would give her a restroom break and she felt unappreciated. The Non-Food Manager came to her rescue and got someone to relieve her. He then saw the 50 million cashiers walking and standing around doing nothing and sent every one of them home.

As of Monday, we lost Overnight Food Specialist.

He was the Non-Food manager, but was switched back to Food Manager because his girlfriend, one of his Non-Food ticketers, suggested the switch because she thought the Food Manager didn't know how to manage Non-Food. He and his girlfriend constantly fought with the Senior Merch. But because the Non-Food Manager and the GM are best friends, they never get in trouble for it. The Merch would fix them by piling extra work on them. And that is fitting because all they did was talk to each other all night and find places in the club to kiss and grope each other. They even fixed it so they would have the same days off. And the GM never knew.

Eventually, their antics affected operations, so I warned both of them about it. To make a long story short, they both survived the meeting senior management had with them about it, and the fact that HR had got involved. Later, he got suspended due to the accusation that he got his girlfriend's card and clocked her in one night. And he did it right in front of a ticketer! Knowing

MONKEYING AROUND

him, he treated the suspension like a vacation. He probably lied to his wife and told her he was suspended for damaging something with his forklift. We don't know if it was a paid suspension, or not. This week, exactly one day before he was to return, the company let him go.

The Merch has now put the pressure on us ticketers to help the remaining specialist to finish on time. I've had my forklift license for over three months and still haven't been paid for it. Our soon-to-be Food Lead was supposed to get certified in November, but management excuses keep delaying it. Other potential drivers don't want to drive because they know I still haven't been paid for driving, and I'm one of the top ticketers there. They are big time pimping our Freezer forklift driver so they can keep their budget low and their bonuses high. He has to recover the freezer and dairy, and at times, pack the diary out, unload the 840 truck(s), pack out the freezer, fill the two ice freezers, boom up food, and at times the Back 40 too, plus pick up empty pallets and put them into the pallet truck. And after all of that, he is still expected to finish on time [10pm-6am]. That is phenomenal considering BJ's is his second full-time job. He barely gets any rest before leaving BJ's to go to his primary job in the morning. Club #028 is very small, so it must run full tilt on a small staff.

We have an excellent management staff comprised of senior managers in their early 30's and mids ranging from late 20's to their 40's.

And our Merch is not afraid to do what it takes to make up for the suspension and the firing. He works 14-15 hour days to cover the overnight deficit and then his opening shift.

MONKEYING AROUND

The GM loves working on the floor whether it be in the day or staying overnight to work with us. He was the Regional Manager's "fireman" as a GMIT. And the Zone Vice President would send him as far as GA to help out stores in her zone. He now has his own store, and still prefers the floor to the office.

One thing about our senior managers is they know time managment. They make sure everything and everyone is done on time. Our former Non-Food Manager was a "Russian". He turned his girlfriend into a "Russian" too. He and his girlfriend would play around all night, and then begin rushing near the ends of their shifts to try to make up for lost time, which was a lost cause. Both would try to make it look as if they were working all night before the Merch or GM came to open in the morning.

So doing everyone else's job doesn't always put you in the running for SOM or SOY. And just doing your job doesn't do it either. All I know is senior and mid management gets together and votes on who gets SOM and SOY.

[quote]All I know is senior and mid management gets together and votes on who gets SOM and SOY.[end quote]

You are correct about the meeting. There is no "criteria" to chose from. Someone suggests a name, it is voted on, and that is how the SOM and SOY are chosen.

At Club 028, our SOY is a Maintenace employee who has been with the company about a year. Time with the company does

MONKEYING AROUND

not count. You have to be SOM before SOY though. I was SOY with less than one year with the company. That was when I worked day shift. I work overnight now.

Our SOY has his haters. They wonder how he got it. Believe me, favoritism was not in play. He is reliable, hard working, has a good attitude, and a good work ethic. I was there to see him repaint the food court at 2am, while the rest of the day shift was sound asleep. I was there to see him go aisle by aisle pulling out full pallets so he could sweep and mop behind them. I was there to see him and the PM at 4:30am cleaning the freezer doors. I was there to see him fully recover the freezer to make it look good for the members. And I was there to see him come in at 6am to help pack out the dairy and cooler. Mind you, these were things he did in addition to his regular maintenance duties.

That man earned his SOM and SOY!

Chapter Twelve: Swinging from the Steel

Just about every daytime team member knows how daytime management steals time from BJ's: they hide in their offices, are on their cell phones right in front of everyone and use being on salary as their excuse, come in late when they know they will be the only day manager opening, or outside on smoke breaks. So how do overnight specialists waste company time?

Before their titles changed from managers to specialists, some would come through the back door, walk to their mail boxes to check for any homework they had, and meet with their superiors if they closed. They had to meet with them until they were gone. After everyone left, they would go to the back, sit in the receiving office, and talk for about half an hour. Others waste time talking to overnight team members, slowing them down, and causing them to stay late. And when their bosses press them for the reason why the employees are still there way past their scheduled time, they throw them under the bus, call them slow, or play dumb.

Overnight Specialists also waste company time by dropping unnecessary pallets. This is not an exaggeration. We had a female Overnight Food Specialist who would ride around on her mechanical horse, and when she saw 3-4 cases of a product was missing, she would ride around until she found a single layer to drop to make the pallet whole again. One of my friends nicknamed her Lady Drop A Lot. Her peer from NY was given the title, Sir Drop A Lot. Fans of 90's hip hop will get the name play reference. We got her to stop that after we took pictures, and showed them to her boss. She met her demise when she hit an expensive flat screen television with her mechanical horse, and did not report it. Previously, she got fired for staying far too long past her time. Her employees lobbied for her return, citing she was the hardest working specialist they had. This was the second time she hit something, and didn't report it, so there was no saving her. A couple of years later, her counterpart was shown the door for constant tardiness. The slap in the face was he came to our location one night when one specialist was on vacation, the other two called out. When he went back to his club, he got the 4th of July Special the day before he was scheduled to go on vacation. That was the second time I saw that happen to someone in management. The first time was when a PM was caught forging documents, and was given the 4th of July Special just before her vacation began.

Remember the Produce Specialist at the beginning of the book? He became an overnight specialist later. According to him, his reserve was so clean that a person could throw a football through it, and not touch anything. That was not a figurative statement. He actually did it! A Senior Merchant in training at his club saw it too, and put a stop to it. The guy's identical twin also worked for BJs as an overnight specialist. Both of them were 6'4, built like Greek gods, and looked like male models. He swung from the steel until his Senior Merchant would no longer cover for him with the GM. So one

SWINGING FROM THE STEEL

night, he left a 15 page droplist. Of course, there was no way he could get it done, and was given the 4th of July Special. Two peas from the same pod.

There are standards for how fast you are expected to work at night, but they are rarely enforced. As a result, you have ticketers who spend hours in one aisle. I have names for guys who swing from the steel like King Kong: monkey boys, golden gorilla, and milk men. For example, one milk man would stay in one aisle for four hours. He was expected to work three aisles in 7.5 hours. He would do two, and then a specialist would send someone to help him with the third, do the third for him, or the guy would simply clock out and go home at the the end of his shift. He did it for years with nobody talking to him about it, or giving him a corrective. Had he and the dairy ticketer not been caught punching each other in an out, he'd still be there filling up pails.

One fellow, I call the golden gorilla, would finish his work, and spent the rest of the time patting boxes, pulling bags to the front of pallets, looking up in the steel, requesting more pallets dropped for him, and making signs so he could make his full 40 hours. You see, at BJ's, hourly employees are automatically charged for a 30 minute lunch break if you work six hours, or more. I remember when I worked for Winn-Dixie in 1991, our time clock was to the second. It's decades later, and BJ's time clocks still aren't that advanced. There is no real-time feature to check your hours. Hours update the next day. We punched in and out for lunch at Winn-Dixie, but were not charged for the lunch. That is the reason why managers would flag any excessive lunch times on their reports, and show them to us. They also flagged us if we got overtime. I remember seeing my produce manager use a yellow highlight when he saw I had 40:01 hours. Yes, even one minute over was not tolerated unless management approved it.

You usually cannot become rich from punching a clock. That also applies to those on salary, even if they make bonuses. Yet they continue to stay late, work overtime, or put in long hours and hope for good raises or promotions. Here is my take on this. Getting overtime or staying late on salary can either help you or hurt you. If your superiors ask you to stay late, then it helps you because it helps them. But if you stay late because you want to fatten your pockets, or because you can't get your work done on time, then it hurts you. Superiors know which is which.

Night crew walks around wearing headphones, wearing earbuds, looking at their phones all night, and carrying on conversations with people on the other end who should be asleep. One of the Overnight AP team members, sits in the receiving office all night, as if he was Louie from the television sitcom "Taxi". He is short and shaped like Louie too. His nickname is "Alf" for two reasons. Because he is short, pudgy, and has a pointy head. And because it is a short version of his first name. I can't take credit for that one. An overnight specialist came up with that one. Nobody talked to him or gave him a corrective for playing Candy Crush while on the clock, talking to his girlfriends in the Dominican Republic [by the way, he is married], or watching videos on his phone. His excuse for slacking is he used to go above and beyond until one time, the Loss Prevention Manager gave him a quarter raise. This was years before the universal 25 cent raise. So he started giving them their money's worth to show his disdain.

SWINGING FROM THE STEEL

Oh yeah, there was also the ticketer who used to crawl into the dog bed boxes, and go to sleep. When they finally caught him, they made it possible for him to sleep all day long if he wanted. Those were situations I witnessed. Now look at what bloggers at other clubs saw.

Slackers at Portsmouth's, New Hampshire Store...

I worked at the store # 062, located at 1801 Woodbury Avenue, Portsmouth, N.H. 03801, and what I can tell about the night shift staff is not really positive...

The shift used to start at midnight and finish at 8:00 A.M.

We used to have a half hour break at 2:00 A.M. and another one at 5:00 A.M.

The problem started there with the managers :

Chr Sm *together with* **Jes Fo**, *and* **Fr Du** *used to take at least 45 minutes each break, instead of half an hour !*

That was a waste of time and money for the company !

And the worst fact was that they used to tell a beginner, called **Ni** *o punch them in, so their "over break", would never be noticed.*

By doing that, they were able to be for more time at the break room, watching TV, or outside the building, using drugs...

SWINGING FROM THE STEEL

*The other manager, called **BI Mart**, was connive at that situation, since he always saw what took place, but never said and did anything to stop it from happening.*

And when the guys from the first shift started to come, they simply pretended that everything was all right.

Unfortunately it happens at the B.J.'s Portsmouth, N.H. store and perhaps the superiors of the company do not even know about this situation...

i was hired at a bj's club in NJ after a month long process. i was hired to be a "overnight ticketer". during the interview with the store manager i was informed that i would be the only female and he asked if i could handle that. i said yes i do know how it is. we agreed to a few things for my availability. during orientation the hr lady starting giving me problems about the hours i could work. she then told us that unions are for the "crappy workers" the people that are fat and lazy and can't do their job. i think she forgot that i told her my husband is in the union. he works at a supermarket and is not fat, lazy, or crappy. he works at least 50 hours a week and is thin and very fit. she spent a good 30 minutes trash talking unions. on my first night the guy in charge let me know how "annoyed" he was that i was there considering i can't lift things.. hahaha. i never said that. i even said he should have me do the water and soda aisles but he insisted that i can't handle that. he pointed to some aisles and told me to go "make it look pretty". after my first night i quit. those people are the "crappy workers" . and i only mean those people i dealt with not all bj's workers. what a joke and waste of my time!

***Mtt M**. one of the overnight specialists, sits on his forklift most*

SWINGING FROM THE STEEL

of the night and delegates some of his duties to ticketers so that he has time to chat, then every morning takes credit for the work. Pallet counts don't mean anything because he erases and reduces counts of ticketers and adds them to his own.

Wow! That was terrible! BJs is nothing like WalMart when it comes to having female overnight employees. Recently, one very qualified girl from the dayshift wanted to work overnight, and one of the seniors said she would be a distraction. The girl was one of us at heart, noone tried to hit on her, and she could outdo most of the guys who already worked overnight. And she drove forklifts! One senior refused a female TM's transfer because he didn't want girls working overnight because they would be distractions. Those were blatant federal violations that went unreported.

And yeah, some ticketers get it rough, while others seem to cruise by with no write ups, easy aisles, and few pallets dropped for them.

BJ's Club 167 overnight shift.... I worked there for a few months and came to the realization that the people that do work hard don't get realized. Those who don't even attempt doing any work seem to always get the spotlight, whether or not it is positive or negative. Remember, I was only there for a few months, but what I do recall is that this guy in the freezer would have three or four outbursts in a single night. He always complained about something. I don't know what he was complaining about, but it was deja vu on almost every night. Another person called out half of the time during his first three months. Well it felt like he did. How in the world did he keep his job?

SWINGING FROM THE STEEL

I chose to end the book with the night crew because every Regional Manager and GM call it "the backbone of the club". If there was no one to receive the merchandise, bring it to the sales floor, and keep it replenished, there would be no store. On the other hand, if there was no day shift, there would be no one to keep the stores clean, assist members, ring them up, or sell memberships, which are pure profit for BJ's, there would be no members.

Truth of the matter is the day shift and night crew are symbiotic. One cannot truly exist without the other. But no company as whole understands that, just people who work there. It is the reason Scott Adams can so accurately make fun of marketing versus engineering, and engineering versus sales. He was one of those who faced the work, not an executive at a ribbon cutting or ground breaking ceremony, or an upper middle manager who just sees numbers and data, or someone in middle management who is pushing the agenda of those from levels above onto those on the front lines.

BJ's Wholesale Club is a regional company, not a national one. It does just enough to maintain its foothold in the States you find it. So being #3, earns it a performance review of basically meets expectations.

Resources

The No-Asshole Rule, Robert I. Sutton, Ph.D. (02-20-2007)

1. http://bjsworkers.blogspot.com/2006/12/breaking-wall.html

2. http://bjsworkers.blogspot.com/2006/11/bjs-wholesale-club-pays-233-employees.html

3. http://bjsworkers.blogspot.com/2007/09/bjs-veteran-named-to-new-post.html

4. https://www.washingtonpost.com/news/on-leadership/wp/2016/12/12/he-was-minutes-from-retirement-but-first-he-blasted-his-bosses-in-a-company-wide-email/?utm_term=.caa06f657bf1

5. https://www.whitehouse.gov/blog/2013/11/07/impacts-and-costs-government-shutdown

6. http://journalistsresource.org/studies/government/budget/economic-effects-2013-us-federal-shutdown

7. http://www.law360.com/articles/135013/bj-s-reaches-9-3m-settlement-with-midlevel-managers

8. http://www.hayberlawfirm.com/blog/2014/02/05/bjs-sued-a-third-time-for-same-wage-violation/

9. http://bjsworkers.blogspot.com/2011/01/happy-new-years-from-bjs-now-youre-laid.html

SWINGING FROM THE STEEL

10. http://www.usatoday.com/story/money/2016/05/18/q-new-overtime-rule/84537486/

11. https://blog.dol.gov/2016/05/18/who-benefits-from-the-new-overtime-rule/

12. http://www.cheatsheet.com/automobiles/11-of-historys-most-infamous-automotive-scandals.html/?a=viewall

13. http://sports.yahoo.com/news/larry-bird-always-knew-his-style-of-play-would-break-his-body-215058486.html

14. http://www.runnersworld.com/runners-stories/a-few-words-about-running-from-the-great-larry-bird

15. http://www.cnbc.com/2017/01/08/intel-ceo-reveals-how-he-almost-got-himself-fired-25-years-ago.html

www.ingramcontent.com/pod-product-compliance
Lightning Source LLC
Chambersburg PA
CBHW061440180526
45170CB00004B/1487